OFF THE BEATEN TRACK

OFF THE BEATEN TRACK

by

D. B. PLUMMER

HILLHEAD PUBLICATIONS

I dedicate this book to Barry Cockcroft of Yorkshire Television with whom I spent considerable time and also to Fiona Richmond with whom I spent no time at all – more's the pity.

ISBN 1 871968 15 1

Hillhead Publications
East Mey
Caithness
Scotland

Printed and bound in Great Britain by
Biddles Ltd, Guildford and King's Lynn

Contents

HARRY'S CROW

—1—

The Gherkin Hunters

I WENT TO SEE the film *Dirty Harry* the other night, but it turned out to be a bitter disappointment. It transpired it was about a way-out cop, played by Clint Eastwood, beating eight bells and a bit more out of a twenty-four carat weirdo with a penchant for locking up young girls. It's not that I don't like Clint Eastwood, I do, but the film wasn't what I expected. Come to think of it though, Panteg village is hardly a place for Warner Bros to film, and Clint Eastwood would have to be pretty well down on his luck to want to play Harry Teague in spite of Harry's pickle barrel and his talking crow with its somewhat limited vocabulary.

Youth, even my own youth, ruled and regulated as it was by an elderly hypochondriac mother, is a wonderful time. It's part of one's life when summers are always hot, Christmasses invariably white, and every colour and sensation brighter and more vivid than at any other time in one's life. It is in fact the only time in the life of the average man when he can say 'the best things in life are free' and really mean it; and though I must confess I couldn't wait for my sixteenth birthday to up sticks and run away from my village, on reflection, mellowed by age maybe, I don't think I'd have liked to have grown up anywhere else.

Characters abounded in my town, real characters – not the cardboard-cut-out Richard Llewellyn TV type figures, speaking with a ridiculously nasal Welsh accent and interspersing every sentence with 'indeed to goodness', but down to earth, one-off individuals, as near to lunatic as dammit is to swearing perhaps, but characters nevertheless, fascinating and enigmatic as a ship in a bottle. Take for instance the incredible Evan Twp (real name Evan Davies), a retired miner invalided out of the pits when his pony in a fit of pique decided to deal out a swift and unexpected kick at Evan's head, thereby addling Evan's already limited brains and rendering him 'Twp' or barmy. Evan believed he was a railway engine – the 11.34 Raglan from Bridgend to be precise – and while a few unkind souls, irritated by his shunting, petitioned to have him sent to the breaker's yard at Plas Wen Hospital for the Silly, he remained in the village until his death, snorting and steaming – more derailed than deranged, I always thought.

The star of our village however was Ivor Daft (real name Ivor Dent – the daft is self-explanatory). Ivor was a very different kettle of fish, who lurked (Ivor always lurked) around Bala tip, bull terrier on slip, and books obtainable only in Cairo tucked inside his shirt. Yes, hell on cats and children was Ivor, much given to heating pennies for the carol singers and baiting nasty little break-back mouse-traps with Mackintosh's toffees to tempt the sweet-hungry children of the village to try their luck. Ivor told wicked scandalous tales about the locals, evil tales and lies to boot and I was thirty-five before I realised I couldn't catch a very unpleasant venereal infection from touching Mary Tompkins' handbag. I bumped into her once while I was trying to read the *Beano* in Dyers' newsagents, and went into a hasty physical decline until Dad told me not to be so silly. Ivor, you were indeed a fiend in human or nearly human form. It was Ivor Daft who found a meat-stealing cat snaffling his entire week's wartime meat ration (scarcely enough to keep a good-sized hob ferret), and it was Ivor Daft who flung the same cat over Oxford Street roofs where it plunged to earth, rapidly burning up its nine lives as it accelerated streetward at 32 ft per second per second. It was the same Ivor Daft who finding a ram battering down the gates of sundry valley gardens to scrump the scraggy cabbages growing there, drove a six-inch nail through his own gate and found the ram transfixed to it next morning. Yes, a wicked man was Ivor, not a bit like one of those chaps out of *How Green Was My Valley*, or *Fallen Hero*, or anywhere for that matter.

But Evan Twp and even the incredibly ferocious Ivor Daft paled to insignificance compared to Dirty Harry Teague, one-time grocer and crow-expert. Harry was not a native of Glamorgan, but some time during the bad times during the fickle 1920s he had come to the district from North Wales, though you couldn't blame him for that I suppose. However by halfway through World War II, when I was engaged in living out my seventh year on this planet, he had become well and truly accepted by the natives of the valley. Harry owned a greengrocer's shop, a strange place where the smell of slightly-off cabbages fought a ding-dong battle with the reek of onions which were liquefying into an eye-watering goo. Oddly enough Harry had the audacity to hang a sign which stated 'Fresh Vegetables' in his window but the strange smell emanating from his shop, a perfume which was reminiscent of a compost-heap in full bloom, attested the lie of the sign.

The bays of wartime cabbages, potatoes, leeks and onions were seldom emptied and never cleaned out and fresh vegetables and fruit were simply tipped a top the hoary oldsters until putrescence reduced the bottommost layer of the bays to a slimy ooze, similar to the type found at the bottom of stagnant ponds, an ooze which seeped out into the passageway twixt the bays and the counter, an ooze which Harry chose not to mop up but simply absorb with numerous layers of paper. Each week Harry would appear behind the counter a fraction of an inch taller, and by the time May came around and Uncle Billy paid me sixpence to fetch the sodden decaying newspapers for his bean trench, Harry would tower above his purchasers, gazing down on them, a veritable Goliath of a man and a far cry from the diminutive pixie of the May previous.

However it was not the scent of over-ripe onions, the reek of 'too long at the fair' cheese, the bubbling sticky vileness of last year's King Edwards, or the viperous perfume of senile Granny Smiths which lured infants into his shop. Indeed we had been warned against such bacteriological hell-holes by cartoon films concerning Giro the Germ, an insect-like bacterium of unknown species which lived in dustbins and undisinfected drains and would have run riot in the happy hunting ground of those bays of vegetables. No, it was not the smell of decomposition that attracted us mites but the presence of a pickled gherkin barrel at the front of Harry's counter, and for those who have been spared such delicacies by public health acts too numerous to mention, I'll explain.

Tale has it the preservative fluid in the barrel, a slimy acidic liquid, dark brown in colour and with an eye-stinging pungence, was of a secret formula known only to Harry. It was rumoured that Jennie Beynon, a lady known to be an authority on Polish airmen, once dropped her purse in the mix and though Harry fished around in the liquid with his son's tadpole net, nothing was found, for perhaps the purse had been dissolved by the contents of the barrel. It was also said that once Gladys Nunn, a girl certain to come to a bad end and who went to teacher training college, was splashed by the liquid and suffered from a withering hand but I doubted the tale as all the Nunns were a bit funny anyway – inbred I supposed.

But to Specky Perkins, my tiny, shrivelled, half-witted classmate and I, this gherkin barrel was no ordinary tub of preserved vegetables, but a hole in the ice in some tundra region known only to us, and we, clad in our balaclava helmets, a curious wartime rig which we wore summer and winter alike, were Eskimos poised above the blow holes of seals awaiting the air-seeking appearance of the gherkins. Deep, in the acidic fastness of the barrel, down in the depths of the slimy ooze a bubble would herald the rising of one of the gherkins, which roused from its sleep like a Kraken, would flash to the surface for a moment before plummeting back into the depths to escape the lunges of our meat-skewer harpoons, vinegary spume splashing our clothes, our skin, our hair, while overhead like the raven of Odin fluttered Harry's crow squawking its only party piece 'Bugger All, Bugger All' as it fluttered from perch to perch leaving nasty smears of whiteness on the caulis (3d each, 7d for 2 – a baffling sales gimmick) and the cheese.

'Don't damage them too much boys,' shouted Harry, driving the crow off a particularly poisonous package labelled Rissole Mix (a brand known to be fatal to crows and men alike I believe), 'I got to sell the buggers' and the crow, encouraged by Harry's prompt, went into a medley of Bugger Alls. 'Crows is not as good as parrots' said Specky, 'All crows can say is Bugger All, but you can teach a parrot to say Arsehole' and Specky began impersonating his disgusting Uncle Gongo's parrot so loudly that Mrs Rees the undertaker's wife rushed across the shop and threatened to wash his mouth out with soap. To my memory we never succeeded in catching a gherkin in spite of our efforts, but day in day out twixt the end of school and the time when Harry shut up his emporium for the night we would be perched above the barrel stabbing at the gherkins and uttering Eskimo sayings.

'Why does he always smell of vinegar?' asked Dad, sniffing at me over the top of his *Daily Worker*. 'It isn't natural for a boy to smell like that, there's something wrong with him. Hell, I can't stand to be near him at the table' and Dad stormed out to the Royal Hotel to savour and enjoy even more pungent vapours. Mam however was too preoccupied with her latest imaginary illness to heed Dad's comments, for Mam suffered from an odd malaise found only in China and caused by the intake of too much rice and fish, so I doubt whether either parent ever found out the source of the bitingly vinegary smell.

Gherkin hunting was a short-lived pleasure however, for it was terminated one day by an angry outburst from Harry and a subsequent ban from the shop. That morning Harry's crow disappeared and Harry suspected Specky of the theft. 'Own up you little bugger,' (we waited in vain for the answering chant of Bugger All, Bugger All) 'you stealed that crow'. 'No, no, Mr Teague', blurted the half-witted Specky, 'I hate crows and my Mam wouldn't let me have one 'cos they do poos on the cheese.' But protestations were useless and that day we were banned from Harry's shop and sent out into the chill of the spring evenings to stare, noses against the window panes, as bubble after bubble rose from the depths of the barrel to burst with a 'plop' on the surface of the vinegar and yet another denizen of the deep rose and sank back into the sticky ooze. To make matters worse Specky and I were wont to slide old verdigried pennies down into the barrel where, often residing on the bottom for a few weeks they emerged mint-fresh, burnished by the unspeakable nastiness at the bottom of the barrel, and that spring Specky and I had speculated a whole four pence on the project. It's amazing but copper salts are very poisonous, yet no one seemed harmed through eating those gherkins pickled as they were in a mix that would have delighted the heart of any toxicologist. Perhaps valley folk are immune to copper poisons in the same way as they seem prone to spina bifida; or perhaps gherkins, like pearls in wine, have some magical property which annuls the effect of all known poisons.

Summer passed slowly and miserably for Specky and I, as we sought out ground-nesting skylark chicks and caught up tiny white-spined baby hedgehogs in Llanpant churchyard, but it was a poor substitute for hunting the gherkins in Harry's shop. We passed his window each day gazing wistfully at the barrel, noting that Harry had devised a new sales gimmick to sell his wares and a sign which now read 'Savoury Gherkins' rested on the hitherto unlabelled barrel. Mam also noticed the improvement in the taste and quality of the gherkins after Specky and I were restrained from stabbing them and commented on how much sweeter the gherkins tasted that summer. Perhaps our lunges at these warty monstrosities did spoil them, and now allowed to surface and plummet in peace they developed the true pickled gherkin taste.

Each day however, I tapped politely on Harry's door, mindful of our ban and cautious and polite as only an eight-year-old can be. 'Can I empty the barrel Mr Teague?' I asked meekly, eager to retrieve my now mint-fresh pennies, and each day Harry would shake his head regretfully, as if he too secretly regretted the ban. One day however, Harry poked around with his tadpole net and pronounced the barrel gherkinless and ready for E. T. Evans' rubbish dump. We trotted after Harry while Specky chuntered on about how long a clay worm he had rolled during 'sums' that morning (Specky's only claim to academic success were the clay worms he rolled while the rest of us toiled and staggered through Hundreds, Tens and Units, sharebys as wicked a torture as any devised by the KGB). At last Harry reached the tip and upended the barrel, tipping out its viler than vile contents while Specky and I stood quivering with excitement like greyhounds on slips ready to dart in and seize our pennies from the slime, but at the very last moment we recoiled in horror, for quite suddenly I realised what had given these gherkins the delicious savoury taste so beloved by Mam. There in the bottom of the barrel, more moth-eaten in death than in life, preserved like an elk in a peat bog, its beak agape and slime-filled was Harry's crow. 'Poor old bugger,' said Harry rubbing his chin wistfully, 'Poor old bugger', but though the beak was agape as if to attempt a croak, the ensuing mimicking squawk never came.

I returned home only a week ago after a lapse of maybe thirty years and one of the first people I met was Specky. Middle-age had neither mellowed nor improved his looks and he peered at me over the top of his now even thicker pebbled spectacles chortling with glee as he did so while we reminisced on the old days, happier times when the cares of adult life were a million miles away. 'You, you was always dead clever at school,' he chortled, his voice as cracked and inane as ever, a bead of spit appearing at the corner of his mouth, 'and I was only able to make clay worms, remember, remember.' We laughed and suddenly ran out of conversation as one-time friends who have grown apart are wont to do. 'Call in and see me sometime' he shouted, and then drove off in his Rolls-Royce. Somewhere, somehow I feel I have missed out on life!

A BITCH AS WOULD BITE AN 'OLE

—2—

'A Bitch As Would Bite An 'Ole Through A Wall'

BY THE TIME I met Corrington he was old, and like most old people faintly irritating and given to rambling on about his youth and middle years. Now, poised as I am on the brink of middle age myself and able to see the stupidity and pomposity of my earlier years, on reflection I think I treated Corrington badly, sighing openly at his seemingly exaggerated tales, impatiently cutting him off in mid-sentence, when I tired of his stories which any thinking person knew to be lies. Perhaps I felt embarrassed when he rambled on about how he had fought an exhibition bout with Jack Dempsey, the iron-fisted Mannassa Mauler, or how he had killed a man in a knife duel after a dog fight in Sonora had seen off a bad loser's 'poke' and caused him to attack Corrington. Perhaps anyone of twenty-five years of age, who had done little of any note with his own life, is bound to be irritated by the tales of a man whose life had spanned nearly a century, and during his long and eventful life, Corrington had jammed as much as any man into his allotted span. His rich kaleidoscope of a life had seen Vila make his abortive sortie into America from Mexico – a series of raids which have inspired a host of exaggerated spaghetti westerns – and he had witnessed the last of the bare knuckle fights staged in America before the sport had insisted that its athletes wear gloves and become 'respectable'.

Right up until the time he died Corrington had seemed ageless to me, and any attempt at my guessing his date of birth would have gone ridiculously awry. I tried to piece together dates and Corrington's age from his ramblings about the days he had spent in the Americas and come to the conclusion he must have been over eighty; but after a while I simply gave up guessing, and because at the age of twenty-five I considered myself one of the know-it-all semi-intellectuals, I became impatient with the old man's tales, irritated by his meandering account of yesteryear, and perhaps I was openly rude to him when he told his outrageous lies about the past. Now I wished I had listened to him, and maybe written down his tales, for Corrington had much to teach, and I had even more to learn.

Tim had been born in Kerry during the latter part of the nineteenth century, times which had been bad for Irish farmers and crofters alike, so the Corrington's youngest sons upped sticks and left Ireland for harsher climes to mingle with races a far cry from the slow-talking Kerry men. Tim sailed to America, landing in the New York of the 1890s – a wild and woolly town where Italians, Jews, Armenians, Turks, Greeks and Irish, misfits and outcasts from a dozen different lands rubbed shoulders and began to jell into a nation. But whether Tim witnessed the birth of a nation or not is unimportant; what he did see was the creation of a new breed of dog.

The Irish have always been enthusiastic dog fighters and many, despite the fact that dog fighting is illegal, still practise the activity. The Irish breeds of terrier, the Red Devil, the Kerry, the Wheaten and the Glen of Imaal were all bred as working dogs it's true, but given a chance the majority of these dogs would rather fight than eat. The Kerry men were famous dog fighters during Tim's youth, not practising the strictly regulated rules of the London pits, nor were the battles the curious rituals seen in the Black Country, but the rough and tumble terrier versus terrier battles were dog fights nevertheless, and Tim became infected with the love of a 'fast' dog long before he set sail for America.

Thus while the potent mix of human flotsam and jetsam of a hundred races were fusing together to form a nation, so were the breeds of dogs brought in by these immigrant families mingling to form a dozen different breeds. Dog fighters from Glasgow and Lanark brought with them hot-blooded Blue Pauls and Red Smuts; powerful ponderous brutes, weighing over sixty pounds in hard condition, dogs capable of crushing a pig's skull with a bite, a bite which mangled and macerated flesh, bone and blood vessel, a bite which crushed the very life out of tissue. Staffordshire mine-workers and chain makers en route for Pittsburg imported bull and terrier hybrids; fast, furious lightweight dogs, which struck like adders and hung on to their adversaries like limpets, sustaining pain beyond description but refusing to release their awful holds. French immigrants brought hybrid type mastiffs and bulldogs, dogs as at home pulling down a recalcitrant bull or checking the charge of a furious bear or wild boar as in the dog fighting pits; and from this curious mongrel mix emerged the American Pit Bull terrier, a devil incarnate when roused, docile with his owners and their children, but death to other dogs, having the speed of its Staffordshire-bred ancestors, and the awesome crunching mangling crippling bite of the Scottish Blue Pauls and Red Smuts.

The new breed was bigger than the bull terriers being bred in Britain and if the new breed was larger, so were the sums wagered on the outcome of battles between these canine gladiators. Cockney Charlie Lloyd, a flamboyant, brash, fast-talking little man wagered a thousand dollars on such battles during times when a gold-prospecting nouveau riche had money to burn. Thirty, forty, fifty thousand dollars was wagered on the outcome of these grim, silent and bloody battles, and though the dog fighting was declared illegal in the New World, in the wild, lawless boom towns of the West it flourished despite legislation.

Corrington had come to the New World without trade or fortune, seeking work in districts festooned with job signs which stated 'Irish Need Not Apply', but because of his sporting Irish background, because of his love of a fast, hard-biting dog he had found work in the kennels of the men who had bred these fearsome fighting dogs and had journeyed from Mexico to the Klondyke to pit their wards against others so inclined. His accounts of the time were fascinating and tallied with what little I knew of American history, and only his far-fetched tales of killing a man in Sonora and boxing an exhibition bout with the fabulous Jack Dempsey irritated me.

I was working in a secondary modern in Shropshire at the time I met Corrington, a small school more concerned with producing citizens than with academic results, and I was, for the first and last time in my teaching career, relatively happy with my state of employment. For the life of me I can't remember how or where I met Corrington and the chances are that just as Tim had gravitated to the pit-fighting kennels in America, so had the presence of my small pack of working terriers lured him to my shabby little cottage. One day he had probably arrived at the place and the next he had become a permanent fixture, for Tim was that sort of person, and despite his age he seemed to fill the room whenever he came into the house.

I was hunting with a terrier man called Podge Absolem at the time, a sleazy, greasy, nasty sort of person, but Absolem owned a van and I had no transport. Hence I tolerated his nasty little sexual sense of humour, his grown-old-teddy-boy disposition, his brown and malformed teeth and his loud mouth, if only to be driven to suitable ratting places where I could use my team of terriers.

Corrington also disliked Absolem, but Tim too had problems. Some time in the early nineteen hundreds he had married an Irish girl and returned to Britain, and now as a widower he lived with his eldest daughter, a dried up shrewish sort of woman desperate to be respectable – so respectable in fact that she denied she had been born in America and coloured visibly when her father came out with one of his tales of the goings-on in the Klondyke, where men were men, and women in desperately short supply. Her husband, a Bob Cratchet type bank clerk, nervous, and immaculately dressed even when gardening, also found the old man an embarrassment; and slowly but surely they found ways to ensure Corrington was driven from the house to spend his remaining days in the reading rooms of libraries, in pubs and at the houses of those who found his stories interesting enough to tolerate the old chap's ramblings. Hence Tim also put up with Absolem's slick tongue and nasty little habits.

So it seems as though I have fulfilled all the requirements of a storyteller and introduced the characters of my story and all that remains is that I must now relate the tale. I was returning from a rat hunt one Sunday morning travelling in Absolem's van when we found an elderly couple waiting outside my house with a roly-poly bull terrier bitch puppy on a lead, and carrying all the accoutrements of a 'free to a good home puppy': a dog basket, a rubber bone and a dog brush. It's curious but the general public seem to regard anyone who keeps dogs, be they poodles or working dogs, as 'dog daft', willing to accept any canine waif and stray dumped on one's doorstep; and over a period of years I have been offered and I confess I have refused an incredible selection of dogs ranging from Samoyeds and Basenjis to an assortment of mongrels which would have done credit to Battersea Dogs' Home. Some of their owners had tried to cut their losses and offered their liabilities at a nominal price, others had been only too desperate to get rid of their wards and would have given them free of charge, but all these unwanted dogs were dogs which were out of control, fractious dogs; dogs grown neurotic because of the behaviour of equally neurotic owners, powerful, aggressive dogs whose owners had bought them as image-makers, only to find out that a spiritual and mental tug of war had taken place between dog and owner – a tug of war in which the dog was clearly the winner. We pulled up the van opposite the very prim and proper couple and I turned to Absolem predicting what I knew was the reason for the presence of the couple at my cottage 'Can you take her?' I whined, 'She's grown too much for us. She's savage, we can't control her' I mimicked. I knew what to expect, at least I thought I knew what to expect. 'Are you the dog man?' the staid and respectable navy-blue-suited man inquired, (dog man – a term I hate actually), and before I could answer his homely little wife chimed up 'We want to find a home for Sophie.' She gestured to the fat puppy at her feet, which was writhing like a maggot in the excitement at hearing her name mentioned. I smiled knowingly at Absolem at the result of my prediction and awaited the inevitable 'We can't control her' but the comment never came. 'We want rid of her,' chipped in the husband, 'she's not at all what we expected of a bull terrier. She's got no go about her at all, useless. Cowers from other dogs, wets herse'n if a dog comes near her and yesterday she ran away from our Mother's kitten. That capped it. I can tell you, ran away from a kitten' he repeated disdainfully. 'We phoned the breeder, if you can call him that,' he added bitterly, 'but he wouldn't return our money nor have the bitch back, so you can 'ave 'er free of charge or we're putting her down.' I glanced down at the excited six-month-old puppy at my feet and back at the indignant little man. 'No go about her' he had said, a euphemism for 'She won't attack, rip and maim every dog she sees', and quite suddenly I realised why the pair had bought the bitch. A vision of the couple visiting friends, Sophie on leash, flashed through my mind, with this quiet, puny, timid little man gaining status by being able to say 'Yes, they're fighting dogs you know, bred to kill. None gamer', thereby gaining a little in stature amongst his friends, becoming perhaps a little more masculine in the eyes of his dowdy, homely, sexless little wife. 'Ran from a kitten' he repeated, touching the bitch a little too sharply with the toe of his shoe to be kindly, and thus, because of my sympathy for the silly, sycophantic puppy on the end of the lead, I became the owner of a bull terrier puppy, Sophie by name and with the proverbial 'as long as your arm' pedigree. It was my first bull terrier, and it will surely be my last.

Absolem was still at my cottage when Tim arrived that evening, and Corrington's eyes lit up when he saw the bitch. We knew what to expect and Absolem cast a pitying glance upwards and shook his head in dismay as once again we were told the story of the Sonora dog fight and the subsequent homicide, followed by the 'is there any man in the audience willing to box a round with Jack Dempsey' tale. Tim went over to the writhing, licking puppy, handling her lovingly, tenderly and as expertly as a violinist would handle a Stradivarius. 'Tis a fine bitch Brian, fine, and one that will "go", believe me.' At the moment Sophie looked anything but a bull terrier which, as Corrington put it 'would go' as she endeavoured to climb up his tweedy jacket and lick Tim's aged and wrinkled face. 'The old bastard's senile' sneered Absolem, as Tim went on about the fighting potential of the pied, portly little puppy, which was desperately trying to perform appeasement gestures in front of Absolem's two surly Bedlington terriers, who lips curled, teeth bared, were menacing the puppy. Tim glanced up at the greasy sneering face of Absolem and began to recite the Walsall poem of the dog fight in Sewerage Street, a poem the highlight of which is the description of one of the combatants: 'And under his arm the pride of 'em all, a bitch as wud bite an 'ole through a wall.' We'd heard Tim recite the poem a hundred times or more and I too had laughed at the incongruous way Tim had tried to recite a Black Country poem with his Irish brogue. 'One hell of a dog, Brian me boy, and if I was you or maybe twenty years younger meself I'd fight her.' 'Fight her – he'd beat her' sneered Absolem sarcastically. 'Ah she's little yet,' went on Corrington, 'a young 'un, but it's a bitch like this that "goes" and that's a fact.' He glanced at her papers, a pedigree on which the red-lettered champions were noticeable by their absence. ''Tis a line not bred for the show bench,' Tim explained, 'she's bred to fight, not to look the part.' Absolem was smiling again, sneering and showing his broken brown teeth. 'You just wait,' said Tim gently 'she's a baby yet, one day she'll grow up and chew up those poodle dogs of yours.' He gestured disparagingly at Absolem's Bedlingtons and I felt Absolem stiffen in anger at the rebuke. 'Senile old bastard,' he sneered, 'he's ready for the old folks' home.' 'She's only a baby yet,' Tim was whittering on, 'one day she'll wake up and all hell will break loose.' Absolem was making 'screwy' gestures behind Tim's back, and I must admit I too began to doubt Corrington's knowledge of fighting dogs.

Frankly I didn't want a bull terrier and on reflection I can't think why in hell I took her in. I've never been an enthusiast of dog fighting and was so deeply committed to my team of rat-hunting terriers that I had no time for any other breed. Sam, my stud terrier, was a young dog in those days and had just sired a fine litter of working terriers. They were a month or so younger than Sophie, but demons each and every one of them literally begging for work and going out of their way to be unpleasant to each other. Adolescence is a difficult time for young lads, but particularly for terrier puppies, for there are constant battles taking place amongst litters of terriers starting to develop their permanent teeth, ridiculous fights triggered off by inconsequential events, but fights which frequently end in the death of one of the litter if one isn't careful about kennelling arrangements.

Of the three puppies, the two males Drum and Heron were perhaps the most evil-tempered puppies I've ever bred, for the smallest action triggered them off into paroxysms of rage against each other and they had only to see one another to be at each other's throats, setting about each other with such frenzy that it was impossible to exercise them together. Myra their sister, a bitch I'd named after my great grandmother, was a wicked opportunist with more brain than either Drum or Heron, and would wait for the outcome of a battle twixt her brothers before pitching in and setting about the loser. I'd intended to rat the team together hoping that once they'd been rat-hunting they would unite against a common foe and forget their differences. As it was they did unite against a common foe. Sadly that foe proved to be Sophie.

Sophie was house-trained and lived in, and because of her close connection with me she incurred a feeling akin to jealousy from the rest of the puppies who watched her from the kennels quivering with excitement as Sophie raced around the run, rolling on her back giving appeasement gestures in front of the cages of any dogs which looked like menacing her. Heron, Drum and Myra simply watched the silly fat clown of a puppy, silently, quivering with an emotion which could best be described as a hybrid twixt excitement and blind hatred for Sophie.

What happened was I suppose inevitable, and occurred so rapidly that there was little I could do to prevent the holocaust which was to follow. One moment Sophie was exercising with Heron who had trounced her once or twice just to show his supremacy and the next Sophie had playfully jumped at Drum's kennel door and caused it to open. Both males forgot their differences and struck at Sophie immediately bowling her, while one fixed her by the face and the other began to work on her soft underbelly. Drum's jaws scarcely covered her incredibly muscular muzzle as he held her down putting in the odd shake or so to increase the purchase of his jaws. Heron however went to work with a vengeance on her soft underside, puncturing her abdomen and sinking his teeth through to her bowels. I kicked them battleless, stamped on them and flung them against the kennels in an effort to save Sophie, but to little avail, and ten minutes later found Sophie scarcely alive, bleeding from a dozen punctures with a dark, foul-smelling wound in her abdomen. I rushed her to the vets', put her into intensive care and hoped for the best. Curiously enough, and I say curiously for most gut wounds kill, Sophie recovered, and henceforth I never exercised her with my other terriers again.

Bull terriers once had excellent reputations as rat-hunting dogs and thus I decided to find some reason to keep this useless ball of blubber. Ratting her alongside the other puppies was clearly out of the question, so I took her out with my veteran ratter, Sam. She must have watched him dig and kill a hundred or so rats, slaying them with deft flicks, but while Sophie seemed most interested and even a little amused at his antics, she showed no inclination to join in the carnage. Once in desperation I tried pushing her head towards a rat which appeared at the mouth of a lair, but the spitting and squealing of the rat so upset my canine gladiator that she screamed and ran back to Absolem's van. That evening I wrote an account of the rat pits for a national paper, an account of a thousand rats killed by a bull terrier dog in record time, but glancing down at the fat, snoring Sophie curled up at my feet, the article was written tongue-in-cheek I fear. I mentioned the incident to Tim of course but he merely smiled and said 'Just wait, the devil will waken her in a few months', and now in the light of what was to follow I wish to God I'd heeded Corrington's warning.

Two weeks later I'd taken Sophie across to a pig farm at a place called Eaton Constantine simply to trade a load of beans I'd grown for twenty pounds of onions. Sophie came along as a matter of course trundling contentedly along behind me and playing quite happily with the five-week-old Tamworth piglets, until the sow had taken offence and had driven the tail-between-legs Sophie out of the paddock. So preoccupied was I with trading my beans for onions, that I failed to notice Sophie was marking a crevice between the pig trough and a concrete meal bunker. I glanced across and saw Sophie wagging her tail ecstatically and snorting down the crevice. 'Bitch marked a rat' my onion-grower remarked, and touched the trough with his thumb-stick. A rat shot out, or at least tried to, and finding Sophie's nose blocking its path, it sank its incisors deep into her leathery snout and hung on. She shot back, rat still gripping her nose, and raced around the paddock squealing. In vain she tried to shake off the rat, frantically battering the creature against the pig trough, rolling on the ground and glancing across at me pitifully as if imploring me to come to her assistance. Then quite suddenly I think I witnessed a metamorphosis, as startling and bewildering as the sight of an ugly gherkin-like chrysalis changing into a gaudy and exotic looking butterfly. Quite suddenly Sophie stopped and took stock of the situation, staring straight ahead, eyes glazed with fear and concentration, while the rat hung from her nose. Then she moved her head slightly to one side and bit, a tremendous bite, the sort which severs another dog's leg, the sort of bite her ancestors had used to cripple, maim and kill monkeys, dogs, bulls and bears. The rat died instantly, reduced to a bloody and furry pulp; but an hour later, my transaction completed and onions on my back, I went to fetch Sophie and found her still shaking that pulverised rat, a creature so macerated that to identify the species to which the cadaver belonged would have taxed the ability of an expert in rodent biology. It was the first time I was to see this fat, comical dog retaliate against any creature or show even the slightest trace of anger. Sadly it was not the last.

What I should have treated as a warning, I ignored, for I was not as well acquainted with the ways of dogs as I am today. Furthermore I don't think I would have heeded Tim's advice concerning the development of fighting dogs, or anyone's for that matter, for I was younger then and because of my youth I thought that there was little I needed to know about dogs. Sophie continued to run free in the yard, carefully avoiding the attentions of my fiery, white-Leghorn cock and generally irritating both the terriers and myself by jumping against their kennel doors and letting their occupants run free. I cursed her for her stupidity, and the released terriers promptly thrashed her, yet she continued to set free the terriers by her sycophantic jumping at the kennel doors. She was invariably covered in a mass of punctures and daily bleeding from a dozen or so bites, but the damned idiot of a dog just didn't seem to learn.

That term, though I was quite happy working at the school and living in the district, I felt rather dissatisfied with my job position. My former college associates visited me from time to time, and each and every one had shed the cloak of the rebellious non-conformist student and become boringly respectable, horribly pompous – and had achieved promotion. I felt very inadequate, stuck on my Scale I post at a rather old-fashioned, rustic secondary modern school with no promotional prospects, and pressured into my only spell of ambition by my friends who were 'going places', I applied for a better job at a very 'with it' comprehensive school some fifty miles away. To my surprise I received a letter inviting me for an interview and in true Plummer fashion I began counting my chickens and working out how and where I could rent a place with enough land to kennel the dogs near enough to the comprehensive school to be able to walk to work. As it happened, it became obvious that I had been invited to the interview simply to make up the number of applicants, and I felt horribly inadequate seated amongst bright young executive type teachers all of whom had the bright predatory eyes of a good promotional prospect. Life to these articulate, smart young men was a moving staircase onto which I was unable to step let alone ascend, and I didn't wait to find out the result of the interview but trudged out of the school gates with the kids, catching a bus home and walking the muddy mile of track to my cottage. Such defeats upset me dreadfully, giving my confidence a tremendous knock, and my spirits plummeted as I trudged up the path to the cottage.

Halfway up the path I suddenly snapped out of my bout of self-pity for Drum lay dead on the edge of the path, his jaws smashed, his tongue protruding from his mouth, his lips curled, teeth bared. At first I thought he had escaped from his kennel and been killed by a motorbike for the land on which my cottage stood was owned by a farmer whose sons were scrambling enthusiasts, but an examination of Drum's neck revealed that he had been strangled to death, for his throat bore the marks of a savage mangling and the tongue which lolled out of his mouth was the blue-black of a chow chow's. There was little time to determine the manner of his death, however, for in panic I raced the half mile to my cottage and pushed open the unlocked door of my kennel yard. The run looked like a battlefield, with pools of blood, urine and frothy slaver speckling the walls of the run and its stone-slab floor. At the edge of the orchard wall lay Myra, her head smashed like a melon struck with a hammer, one eye gazing fishily and obscenely in what appeared at the time to be the wrong direction. I touched her body with my foot for somehow I could not believe that carnage of this nature could take place on my premises, but at the edge of a patch of rough cover lay Sophie, her head buried in a clump of nettles, her pied body speckled with blood and filth. At first I thought Sophie too was dead and the whole bloody carnage was the work of some insane prankster, who not only bore me a grudge, but had set to work on my livestock with a vengeance. But as I approached Sophie, her tail gave an ecstatic wag causing blood to ooze from a dozen punctures near the base of her spine, yet she refused to raise her head from the nettle bed. Her sides were heaving with a curious obscene almost sensual rhythm and as I parted the nettles I saw her eyes glazed with an insane fury staring as though in a trance, her teeth locked in the throat of a bloody and torn mess of what had once been Heron. He was quite dead and rigor mortis had long set in yet Sophie continued to grip the body, every now and then giving the corpse a gentle shake like a poodle playing with a rag doll. I should have listened to Corrington, heeded his words concerning the development of a fighting dog. I'd seen the warning signs, ignored them because I thought I knew best, and now like some blood-maddened Sleeping Beauty the real spirit of Sophie had awoken, wreaking havoc and carnage.

As it was I never told Corrington what had happened for on the eve of my abortive interview, Tim had died suddenly. Larger-than-life characters never sicken and grow ill, petering out like some anaemic Camille. One minute such people are hale and hearty and the next they are dead. Such had been the case with Tim. Bob Cratchet and wife had invited some friends round for tea and Tim, excited by the presence of a new audience, had gone straight away into the lie of the mayhem in Sonora and how he had fought an exhibition bout with Jack Dempsey. His tale had caused great embarrassment by all accounts, with Cratchet and wife colouring visibly, but Tim had pressed on with his yarn telling it with such gusto that his enthusiasm had been the death of him.

I borrowed a respectable looking suit, applied for leave of absence and attended Tim's funeral. Funnily enough he was older than either Absolem or I had thought, but then a man like Corrington crams so much into his stint on earth that it is impossible to date him accurately, I suppose. A blasé parson read a standard sermon over the old chap finishing with a bored, indifferent reading of the 23rd psalm, while I watched two rats scampering and fighting each other in the hedge beyond the open grave, and I couldn't help feeling that Tim would have preferred a few verses of the 'Battle in Sewerage Street' to see him into the hereafter. My mind drifted off to the tales Corrington had told us; white lies, fibs never intended to hurt or to create an image for the teller, but I was snapped back to reality by the parson saying a few words about the old man and his long and interesting life. His schpiel had been prepared by Tim's daughter who stood dutifully and dry-eyed, glancing at her watch from time to time at the edge of the grave while the vicar read a summary which resembled an elegy for a country parson, a bland and boring account of the life of a milksop of a man, not a tale of the giant now residing in the coffin at the bottom of the grave. I glanced across at his daughter and her simpering, half-baked husband and felt hot tears of rage come to my eyes, that they had allowed my larger-than-life hero to be reduced to the ranks of the ordinary. 'Damn you, damn you' I muttered, choking back my anger, but I was never a bold man, never one given to bouts of eloquence, so at the end of the reading I too threw a handful of soil on the coffin and prepared to go home.

Tim's thin-lipped, parchment-skinned daughter stopped me as I passed through the cemetery gates. 'My . . .' she jibbed at calling Tim her father like a pit bull shy of 'making the line' – 'The old man asked me to give you these', she said icily, and handed me an envelope. She turned tail and left the cemetery, her sensible heels clattering on the path. I watched her go, disliking her and all her kind stood for, loathing the pseudo-respectability of these bland, indifferent and stupid people whose orderly lives ran on an even keel, unruffled by excitement, from birth to death, and wondered how in hell the old man had sired such a shrew.

I stood alone in the cemetery after the black-clad crowd had left and opened my envelope, Tim's parting gift to me. Inside was a well-worn programme of an exhibition bout of boxing, featuring Jack Dempsey; and a 'wanted for murder' poster, written in Spanish and printed in Sonora.

DANK'S WHIPPET

—3—

A Shadow of My Former Self

I LEFT ROTHERHAM seventeen years ago, so I wonder whether the natives of that town still think — cemetery is haunted. Some eighteen years ago the place had a hell of a reputation for spooks and things which go bump in the night, and at one time, locals were reluctant to pass that cemetery during the daylight hours let alone after the sun had gone down. Well, seventeen years is a long time – though I am pretty sure the neighbours still remember me – and I doubt whether the police are keen on taking any action about events which took place that long ago; so I'll confess. It was I who was the phantom of — cemetery.

Let's start at the beginning, if I can remember that far back. I suppose the tale begins with meeting one Patrick John Danks, known rather less than affectionately to the police as Paddy Danks. Yes, the tale proper starts when Paddy got 'took' by the police for displaying an interest in church architecture – well, not exactly the architecture as much as the lead flashing which was used on most churches at one time. This when stripped off a building fetches a considerable price when sold to a reputable 'tat yard', as scrap dealers' premises are wont to be called in the district where I now live. Paddy, who was never a clever thief and was described even by his Irish friends as 'a leetle bit tick', had been caught red-handed loading the lead into an old pram which had carried over the years equal quantities of babies and scrap metal, for the Danks were a huge family, so large in fact that people said the reason why Paddy bred so many kids was that he hated his wife and was trying to lose her in the crowd. Paddy as I've said had been caught red-handed, but loudly protested his innocence, screaming 'You are arresting an innocent thief' as they dragged him away to the nick. The story goes that when asked if he required any of his other misadventures to be 'taken into consideration' his statement read like a Sears Roebuck catalogue, and the upshot was that Paddy was whisked away to the nick for twelve months; and from that time all my troubles seemed to begin.

I had been in Rotherham maybe six months when I first met Paddy, and on the night in question, the June moon had made my hunting ground a sea of shimmering silver, which is pretty poetic when one considers I was poaching the Rotherham sewage beds. I'd passed the place for a month or two on my way to work until one day I found a loose strand in the chain-link fencing, and by dint of a quick tug on the way to school, and another on the way home, by March I'd made a fairly sizeable hole in the fence through which I would wriggle with my team of terriers to hunt the rabbits which usually abound around sewage beds. Boy, I had some happy times hunting there, squelching around after the bunnies, and although it was an uncommon event to actually come home with a rabbit my dogs had taken, the sport I had was fantastic. That year some fraud in a northern University was researching a PhD on night-time teaching-staff activities, and I felt such a damnable fraud writing 'chess' on the form this loon handed me. The teaching profession must keep up an air of respectability – I suppose that's why most go round noses in the air, but just now and again the veil slips and something dreadfully seedy about teachers is exposed. The week I wrote 'chess' on his questionnaire and felt ashamed about my sewage bed exploits, a really snooty teacher I met at a conference (which I had been forced to attend) was put on probation for having a mirror device attached to his umbrella and standing next to mini-skirted dollies using his periscope device to look up their clothes. He realised the game was up when he eyeballed a pair of navy blue police-issue knickers I suppose, but then all good things come to an end, and anyway in those days I never worked in a school where there wasn't at least one weirdo with nasty habits on the staff. Back, however, to the more pleasant nights on the sewage beds.

Those sewage beds were pretty unsightly by day, for the whole area was covered in a reddish mist spewed out by a factory opposite, a mist which someone high up in the public health offices had put about was health-giving! By moonlight however, the place was not only beautiful but jumping with rabbits, and on the night in question my terriers were hunting them with a vengeance, racing over the grassy banks, disappearing into beds of solidifying squelch and generally enjoying themselves. Sam, my veteran, who was old even seventeen years ago, put out a rabbit and I saw him hightail after it only to be overtaken by a whippet which appeared from nowhere snapping up the rabbit under Sam's very nose. Turning I saw a scruffily dressed man pocket the whippet's kill and stroll towards me. I prepared for flight, for I am not a courageous sort of bloke at the best of times, and I had no right to be hunting rabbits on that sewage bed, but my new aquaintance extended his hand and said 'Patrick Danks sir' and touched his forelock in respect. My associate was both scruffy and smelly and had a pungence of garden refuse, diesel oil and ferret, attempting but failing to disguise an even stronger body odour. I think I replied, 'Charmed I'm sure', which must have sounded just a little ridiculous, considering I was meeting a scruffy, poaching, lout on a smelly sewage bed, but us Plummers have always had a reputation for being polite – brave never, but polite, yes!

Poachers normally feel very resentful about some other unauthorised person trespassing on their patches. For after all, it was my hunting ground, my ingenuity at unpicking the wire; Paddy didn't even have a piece of the action concerning the creation of the sewage as he lived twelve miles away and had cycled here, whippet in pannier of his stolen butcher-boy bike. But it was literally impossible to be angry with Paddy – for he was just that sort of person. Paddy in fact cycled everywhere not merely to get the exercise, but simply because, on account of his strange and very pungent aroma, the bus company were reluctant to allow Paddy on board. Drawn together by what I hope and pray was an attraction of opposites, we became friends and Paddy invited me home.

Paddy lived in the end house of a little row of terraced houses which were in the process of being demolished, and for some reason the powers that be had decided to leave Paddy's house standing, possibly because of the trouble they would have had rehousing the horde. Horde it was I'm afraid, a sticky, urine-scented band of kids, happy as pigs in you-know-what, of every conceivable type, face and hair colour, the only common link being a strong family trait known as enuresis, which in lay terms means the bladder tends to slyly evacuate itself without any warning. They were a pungent little group, a little lousy certainly, flea-bitten but respectful, gentle and generous beyond bounds, and in spite of the pong I wouldn't have minded a family like Paddy's, a little fewer perhaps, but he didn't have a 'wrong 'un' in the batch.

And what a batch they were; I never actually found out how many kids Paddy had and I rather doubt if Paddy knew either. The locals, unkind as most people are to members of their group who are different – I've had some problems myself – made fun of Paddy and family, making the whole messy, smelly little colony figures of fun. Paddy's wife Rene was deaf, or so the local pranksters said, and when she tumbled into bed with Paddy each night, Paddy would say to Rene

'Do you want to sleep or what?'. To which Rene being deaf would reply 'What' and this accounted for the enormous number of children in the family. Birth control, à la Danks, supposedly consisted of Paddy shouting upstairs on Christmas Morning 'Father Christmas has been', jumping sharply out of the way of the stampede, and keeping the survivors.

The house however had to be seen to be believed. Paddy had to my knowledge never worked, and so little money actually came into the house. Social service handouts in the form of unwanted, out-of-fashion new, and rather tatty second-hand furniture promptly underwent a quick smearing with sticky, syrupy stuff from the hands of numerous infants, and blended in with the rest of the ravaged household furnishings. The house was incredibly smelly, the chairs, walls and rugs being permeated with the ever-present smell of stale children's urine, with just a soupçon of sundry other animals. One of the locals had supposedly seen Paddy carrying a small pig home from a farm one day and asked Paddy where he intended to keep the creature. 'In der kitchen' Paddy had answered. 'What about the smell?' the neighbour asked, 'Pigs don't mind smells' Paddy replied.

My favourite tale of my adventures concerning Chez Danks, was of a visit to Paddy's outside loo, a nasty little bucket-under-board affair, mention of the contents of which should be best left out of a book of this kind. The door swung on one hinge and had no lock, furthermore the Danks girls, totally uninhibited about the bodily functions of family or strangers, turned out in number to watch a stranger use the lavatory, probably curious to see if strangers had the same lavatorial habits as the Danks. I went out to use the toilet one day, saw its swinging door, noticed the absence of the lock and the presence of an audience of Danks infants and returned to the house a little shamefaced. 'Paddy, there's no lock on the toilet door' I said with some embarrassment. 'Who'd want to steal a bucket of shit?' Paddy replied, mystified by my stupidity. Later Paddy was given a trio of tumbler pigeons which he kept in the loo and the door was promptly given a hinge and a lock. It's a question of values I suppose, and it would be a funny world if everyone was the same.

So it was I teamed up with Patrick Danks and we shared each other's hunting places, my terriers working cover and pushing out rabbits, and Paddy's whippet doing its damnedest to catch them. However Paddy's 'patches', his own hunting grounds, were either downright illegal or dangerous. Once he took me on a trip to some building, the land around which was enclosed by Stalag type fencing, and after nosing up the chain link in the manner of a pig pushing up an insecure pig wire, he invited me into the compound. ''Tis an approved school,' I think he said 'or 'tis one of dem maximo securicorp prisons. Anyway ders no danger of getting caught and if you gets caught ders no one going to get to know of it.' Come to think of it I've met quite a few people who go out of their way to poach outrageous places, knowing full well the embarrassment which would result from the publicity concerning a conviction of someone caught poaching in high security places usually prevents prosecution. In fact one of the safest places to poach is one of those high security prisons which incarcerate mass murderers, child molesters, local government officers and similar undesirables.

Poaching the railway embankments however is a whole different ball game, and here it is necessary to digress a little about that mass of baffling complexities known as the English legal system. Basically there are no laws concerning common trespass but there are laws to deal with people who trespass on certain particular places. For instance should a mortal enemy of yours open the front door of your house, walk in around your breakfast table and walk out again, providing he didn't snatch up a piece of toast or similar, there is nothing the police could do about it. However one doesn't need to snatch up a piece of toast, chase a rabbit, shoot a pheasant or attempt to steal a piece of BR fixtures to get prosecuted for trespassing on railway property – just being there is enough, and judging from the number of children who get prosecuted for climbing railway embankments there seem to be no 'let you off this times' and no warnings.

I'm no hypocrite and I confess I've always been in pursuit of rabbits on, under and alongside railway lines, but I'm always careful and I take off like a hare at the first sign of danger. Paddy, however, was a fat little Irishman with arthritic hips, so escape from a pair of pursuing railway policemen was not so much unlikely as impossible; yet to underestimate a man of Paddy's type is not only a mistake, but also very foolish indeed. Now if I can leave behind one single epigram by which I might be remembered when I pass on, it is 'Public officials usually leave a person alone if they consider him stark staring barmy'. The Moslems treat nutters with respect, as they say they have been touched by Allah; likewise police, public health officials, planning officers and even muggers usually give a lunatic a fairly wide berth because they can never be certain what in hell he'll do next. Which is probably the reason why High Court judges are rarely taken to task about some of the incredible judgements they make. All the world loves a lover perhaps, but all the world leaves the madman to his own devices is more of a truism. Let me give an example of what I mean, before returning to the story of Paddy and the railway police. Travelling through the tunnels and subways which literally undermine

Birmingham is inclined to be something of a hazard these days, with muggers of all shapes, sizes and hues actually working on a rota system to get a fair whack at Johnny Public. One chap called Charles Stevenage, a lay preacher/actor, who is to self-defence what Danny La Rue is to heavyweight boxing, was chanced on by a band of black boys just a month ago, but when they accosted him, demanding money with threats of the boot going in if none was forthcoming, Charlie suddenly found his acting skills really useful. On the first gentle kick from a pair of oversized Doctor Martins, more of a free sample than a threat, he promptly burst into song, giving them three verses of 'Jesu', Joy of Man's Desiring' and inviting them to join him in the chorus. A startled look swept over the faces of the belligerent band who glanced at each other, panicked and hightailed it out of the subway. Meanwhile back to the railway embankment and Paddy Danks.

We were working a patch of railway line twixt Holmes and Tinsley, a place equally well frequented by railway police as rabbits, and ferreting the embankment in fine style – nets in place, dogs marking and a ferret down. Suddenly out of the blue a railway policeman appeared and began to trot towards us. I panicked I admit, but though I had never really admired Paddy's IQ he was far from 'tick'. 'Run fer it' he gasped, 'You'll lose your job if you are caught' and having said this he waddled toward the railway policeman while I hurled myself into cover. Paddy stood stock still while the burly brute read the riot act and prepared to take down Paddy's name and address, when quite suddenly Paddy took his own hand out of his pocket, bit it savagely drawing blood and equally suddenly burst into tears, showing the astonished railway bobby the damage inflicted on the messy, dirty, blood-stained hand. I will never forget the look on the officer's face – a mixture of blank disbelief and panic would scarcely be adequate to describe it. He put his notebook away, backed off from Paddy returning to his car, and I watched him mime the incident for the astonished officer in the car. For a minute they stood looking at Paddy shaking their heads as if in amazement and finally drove off. 'Get der nets up and let's get to your house and clean up dis hand' whispered Paddy.

However, no amount of hand-biting or histrionics proved sufficient to get Paddy off the lead-stealing incident, and just before he went down he visited me and asked me to look after his whippet during his imminent spell of incarceration at one of Her Majesty's establishments. 'I'm afraid Rosemarina will touch it', he confessed. Rosemarina Danks, a ten-year-old unlovely child with a constant stream of sticky spittle running from her mouth, an unhealthy trace of impetigo, and reputed to carry germs unknown to the bacteriologist, had according to Paddy 'seen off' his rat-fed litter of ferrets by simply touching them and Paddy wasn't prepared to take any chances with his beloved whippet. Hence I became the temporary owner of a shy, nesh, fawn-and-white little whippet, frail of form, gentle of disposition, but a 'killer' with rabbits.

It's said that nature abhors a vacuum and likewise so must have 59 Clarendon Street, Rotherham, a nasty little-two-up-and-two-down house where I lived out some two and a half years of my life, for no sooner was one nutter whisked out of my life when another appeared as if by magic to take his place. No sooner did the clang of cell doors sever my relationship with Paddy than one Alex Kirk, an out-of-work artist, began knocking on my front door looking for a place to stay. Alex was the exact opposite of Paddy, a fastidious, rather effete young man who kept his nails immaculate and considered he was roughing it if he had to forfeit the soup during a three-course meal. Such a curiosity was doomed to have a very short life span at a house such as mine, a house which Paddy incidentally considered was luxurious. Indeed, never were a pair of people so totally different, and the only thing Paddy and Alex had in common was that both considered 'work' a four-letter word.

Alex had lived in a cosy little semi-detached on the other side of Rotherham with his elderly respectable mum and dad, who had tolerated their work-shy guitar-carrying son for some twenty odd years, after which they issued an ultimatum, get a job or get out. Hence Alex, like a true pioneer, saddled up his hi-fi and journeyed west to 59 Clarendon Street to seek less demanding, if not greener pastures, and possibly see how the other half lived, before returning home to Mummy, tail between legs, to beg forgiveness and to take a job selling gents' shoes, a job he considered beneath him, as incidentally, he considered any form of permanent employment. Actually Alex was pretty typical of the type of person produced by art schools during the early sixties, schools which turned out discontented young lads and lasses by the bucketful, kids equipped only with the ability to paint completely abstract and daft pictures consisting of lines and blobs which would not have taxed the artistic ability of a good chimpanzee. Thus equipped, and given just a few lessons in some equally obscure philosophy, they were thrust totally untrained, completely inadequate and extremely pretentious into a never-had-it-so-good early 1960s era, which allowed, if not encouraged, people like them to exist. Today's youth have experienced the bite of genuine hardship, but in those days the educational establishments from universities to art schools went out of their way to produce useless malcontents, which the workers – and there were still jobs in those days – laughingly labelled beatniks and supported not only willingly, but happily. Alex had had an easy life and the only trauma he had ever experienced was when one of the unemployed at the dole office had broken Alex's guitar because Alex had refused to play 'Bless This House' – a comment which Alex had refused to find amusing.

Alex was horrified at how the other half lived on my side of town. The outside toilet almost made him resolve not to defaecate, the absence of a bathroom which necessitated frequent, or rather infrequent, expensive trips to the Rotherham public baths filled him with dismay, but what really upset Alex was the fact that the communal backyard shared by four houses had a 'Nade'. Perhaps I'd best explain what a Nade is. In the yard lived a family of somewhat addled-brained people who specialised in producing weird and peculiar children, one of whom was christened Anthony, so I believed, but his mother unable to say Anthony was wont to call the little monster 'Anthonade', which in time was shortened to 'Nade'. Now, no slum property should have a communal yard without a Nade for the presence of such a creature encourages people to save up their spare cash and get the hell out of such places. In fact on reflection it is my considered opinion that the Rotherham Housing Department had a set of Nades on their payroll for just that reason.

Nade's little forté which upset both Alex and I was to stand on my outside window-sill and urinate down the pane. We asked his mother to stop him performing this horrid little caper, but our pleas did no good. Furthermore, when Alex would whip back the curtains as the little wretch was performing and brandish a pair of shears, indicating their snipping action, the gesture gave us only a short respite, and next bladder-emptying time would find Nade up there performing for all the world as if nothing had happened. Just now and again Alex in desperation would find mother and Nade in the yard and offer the child a sweet from a Warfarin rat poison packet, but even this had little deterrent value and Nade continued to perform three or four times daily, or more often in cold weather.

Funnily enough, the rest of the yard found nothing offensive about Nade's little habits, but complained bitterly and often about the presence of my lurchers, terriers, ferrets, and worst of all about Alex. Seldom did a day pass when a planning officer, a policeman or a public health chap did not knock on my door to complain about something, and while I admit neither Alex nor I were ideal neighbours, I think we took a lot of unnecessary persecution.

Well, to get to the point of the tale, deterred from entering the yard by the withering, sill-destroying rain from Nade, I decided to make the big break and rent an allotment conveniently, though somewhat ghoulishly, situated next to the cemetery. I was to prepare myself for the self-sufficiency leap southwards to Huddlesford, by planting potatoes and keeping some rather mongrelly scrub chickens in the pen which abutted the cemetery. I wasn't happy at No 59 and come to think of it the neighbours weren't exactly happy about having me there. The previous tenants of the property had been pillars of the community so it seems, going to whist drives on Saturdays, bingo twice weekly and living as all proper folk should, so the presence of a ferret-keeping lunatic didn't exactly do a great deal for the other dwellers whose houses overlooked the communal yard. Things got a little out of hand when I fed a dead cat (a road casualty I found in Kimberworth) to my ferrets, and had a visit from our local bobby who was now thoroughly fed up with the goings-on at No 59. 'I understand you feed dead animals to your ferrets' he mumbled as I opened the door, but when I explained it would really be cruel if I fed these animals alive he was thrown a little and walked off to the station shaking his head, baffled by the complexity and ambiguities found in Moriarty's Criminal Law no doubt.

Well, matters came to a head a week later and boy, do I mean came to a head. I've never been much of a dab hand at any form of craft; wood-work leaves me cold, I hate working in brick, and I'm not too hot at concreting either. However some time during the winter of my last year in Rotherham I bought an electric motor, fitted it with a tungsten carbide wheel and began to fashion knives out of scraps of steel I picked up at the local tat yard. At first the knives resembled early attempts at metalwork by the pupils of a school for the mentally handicapped, but after a while I became proficient enough to make swords for the local amateur dramatic society's production of *Macbeth* (see my book *Artisan Hunter*, there's a great tale about this). Well, one day I got lucky, though in the light of what followed perhaps lucky isn't really the correct expression. That day I came on a bluish piece of metal heavier than the usual mild steel or cast-iron, which turned out to be the result of a discontinued experiment at case-hardening steel. Nothing seemed to scratch it, it refused to bend under the most awesome pressure and was totally free from stress cracks. It was in fact perfect for the making of a skinning knife, the sort which would see off a grizzly bear, or at a pinch, Nade.

However, the metal turned out to be like one of those unbreakable toys a parent gives a child at Christmas; a toy which proves to be indestructable but allows the child to destroy every article of furniture in the house by dint of thumping it with the toy. Nothing could cut the damned steel, and though I shaped a roughish sort of knife with an acetylene cutter, I had hell's delight shaping and finishing it on the wheel. Sparks flew everywhere, in my hair, on my clothes, and also on the floor which was covered with a layer of shavings, the result of an abortive attempt at fashioning sword handles for the Macbeth fiasco. In next to no time the cellar began to fill with smoke and the shavings began to glow ominiously. I think I panicked but I can't quite remember, for quick as a flash Alex raced down the steps and poured the dregs of a cask of beetroot wine he had made over the conflagration. There was a hissing and a spluttering and, before I had chance to congratulate Alex on his ingenuity, the house began to fill with a strange incense-like smoke of the type produced by makers of Dorothy Lamour type films about the mystic east. A sweet, cloying vapour filled the house, a smoking perfume which had an odd purple tinge about it. Sadly it filled not only my house but also seeped in next-door via the hole through which fitters had driven the gas pipes. We opened the windows, banged the doors and tried a million methods of dispersing the vapour, but it remained steadfast, a choking perfume which tainted the tea we drank for several days after the conflagration.

A banging on the front door brought us out of the stupor induced by the fumes and we found Mrs Buckmoor a next-door neighbour standing there, a formidable harridan of a woman, hair in curlers and spittle dampening the corners of her mouth, as she prepared herself for the outburst which was to follow. 'What are you doing! What are you doing! We're sick of you and your madness. Barmy that's what you lot are, bloody barmy. The smoke has ruined a big leg of pork for me, ruined it', she gestured with her hands to indicate the size of the leg, a leg more suitable for propping up the corners of a mammoth rather than a pig. I was about to apologise profusely and offer to pay for the meat – on HP if possible as things weren't so good at that time – when Alex, who had had enough of Nade, the complaints, Mrs Buckmoor and more Nade, exploded. 'How dare you' he nearly shouted, 'How dare you', and the awesome Mrs Buckmoor who had never known retaliation from either of us staggered backwards as if struck in the face. 'How dare you' boomed Alex, elated by his initial success. 'We would never dream of interfering with your religious services,' (Mrs Buckmoor was a sort of bingoist-cum-baptist) 'and now you deny us our ceremonies, our rights to conduct a religious service.' She took one step back and the spittle at the corners of her lips shot back into her mouth. 'You nutters,' she hissed, 'you bleeding nutters', but Alex was in full flight by now and was on to seeing the race relations people about her so he couldn't have noticed the warning signs.

The walls of the houses in Horridsville were paper thin and allowed no privacy whatsoever, and there was a tale told locally of the Jerry building which allowed such places to be constructed. A little girl knocks on the door of one of the houses and tells the lady of the house that the picture nail the lady has driven into the wall has come through into the child's house. 'Oh, you're from next-door', the lady says apologetically, 'No, next-door-but-one' replies the child. Well, things weren't quite that bad, but we could hear everything Mrs Buckmoor was saying about us to her much-bullied husband Joe, a great fat gentleman, who wanted to leave his wife, but just couldn't summon up the courage to go. 'Go and 'it 'em Joe, give 'em a beating – that's what they need, burning all that "incest" next-door. They got no right to do that not in a terrace. 'Snot right, 'snot normal, 'it 'em Joe 'it 'em', but Joe would give a quick belch and settle back into his chair to watch *Match of the Day*, oblivious to the pagan rights taking place next door. Alex however was given a new lease of life by overcoming the terrible Mrs Buckmoor and soon went just that little bit too far.

One day Alex heard Mrs Buckmoor trundling down into the cellar to put a shilling in the gas meter and inspired by his early success in his war with her he went into yet another flight of fancy which was to top the lot, 'incest' as well! Alex, realising he had an attentive audience next-door, went into fourth gear at once. 'Oh mighty Legba, Lord of the Earth and the Skies,' ('Joe the buggers are at it again, come and listen. Wake up Joe come and listen') 'God of all Gods,' Alex went on, 'Master of the Darkness' ('they're at it Joe, come listen') 'We give thanks for the fertility of our crops' (our potatoes were just coming up at the time) 'and the infertility of our women' ('they're talking about women Joe, talking about women') 'You, oh Legba, who have refused our offerings of incense and of grain, to you we offer this new-born babe,' (absolute silence from the Buckmoors, or at the most a horrified hiss) 'this we offer to you' – scream from Alex, a roar of Panda cars, and that was it, police, public health council officials, Alex out, ferrets out, dogs out and me trying to look nonchalant sharing the allotment shed with six mongrel hens.

Things weren't too good at school either and my Dickensian headmaster, pin-stripe suit and pin-sized brain, was engaged in a moral struggle with his alter ego as to whether he was to allow sex education and data about sexually communicable diseases to permeate the rest of the useless crap we were serving up under the guise of education. At last he resolved the moral issue after a titanic battle twixt progress and what he knew to be morally right, and called a staff meeting trying to sound like a Moses about to dish out ten good pieces of advice. 'I have decided' he pontificated 'that we must teach the children, the children' he repeated, to sound really pious, 'that venereal disease, which' he emphasised 'is caught only as the result of chance sexual encounters, is God's way of ensuring that temporary sexual relationships are abhorrent to Him.' Foolishly I offered up a similar theory about Hansen's disease, which is only transmitted after constant contact twixt people, suggesting it was God's way of ensuring marriages didn't last. There was a deathly silence as Miss Pilger, his senior hatchet-woman, wrote something on her note-pad. Shortly after I was summoned to the head's room and placed on the transfer list so to speak. It's difficult to sack a teacher, very difficult in fact, and providing one doesn't sexually assault a child or worse still make a mistake in a register, a person can stay on for life at almost any school. Well, not quite, for the powers that be, working undercover a little, have curious ways of getting rid of unwanted teachers, simply by making life so hot and unpleasant that an unwanted teacher ups and leaves. Tops on the list for making things hot is to give a teacher an uncontrollable class composed of Hieronymous Bosch type kids, capable of driving a sensitive teacher nuts. However I already had such a class full-time and was already nuts, so I was simply 'phased out' as the saying goes, which the head probably put down to being God's way of punishing teachers who keep ferrets. This phasing out is a neat little piece of ostracising which is brought about by the head encouraging the rest of the staff and kids to act as if the teacher in question doesn't exist. Curiously it works, and produces a state of depression second to none; and is one of the reasons why many teachers get nervous breakdowns. It's a bit petty perhaps, but then so are many teachers.

All this action did for me was to make me turn more and more towards the world of hunting, of chasing rats in and out of cadavers at maggot factories, and to make me generally prepare myself for the stint of unemployment which seemed inevitable now that the head was hotting up my spell of being sent to Coventry. Each school day would abruptly end at 4.00 p.m. and I would race home to let out the terriers and hunt a few rats. Each night I would put the dogs away, bed them down, and settle into my own bedroom separated from the hens by a wire netting partition. I tried to retaliate against the neighbours once and only once by placing a poster in my front room window which stated 'This house to let to large musical family of Jamaicans only' but the police made me take it down, so after that I gave the world a miss and just let things roll over me.

Well, one night I returned home after a particularly fruitless night rat-wise, and for no particular reason flashed the beam of my torch around the cemetery. The place was alive with eyes glowing like coals in the darkness, but the eyes were not the ghosts of folk long past, but simply those of rabbits which usually abound in most graveyards, for rabbits and other denizens of the British countryside don't get excessively hunted in cemeteries. In fact flora and fauna get relatively untouched when living on top of those long departed. The ancients had the wisdom to plant yew in such places, to grow for bow staves, for it seemed unlikely that a medieval vandal or twelfth-century glue-sniffer would wreak havoc on any plants growing in such places – and after this useless piece of information let us return to the rabbits.

I must admit I had some qualms about hunting rabbits in a cemetery, but I confess that it isn't the dead who worry me but their nearest and dearest who would probably take a dim view of a spot of coursing over their loved ones. I wasn't very popular in the district anyway and I was fairly certain that should I be caught hunting rabbits in a graveyard I'd have had a fairly hot reception at the local police station and an even hotter reception at the psychiatrists, for those who deal with the psychologically disturbed are apt to imagine all sorts of odd things about chaps who make night-time sorties into cemeteries.

Still, each night I shone the beam around the graveyard, whippet straining at the leash. 'I know a great name for the owner of a crematorium,' cracked Alex, 'Molten Slumber' but I ignored him, partly because I considered the joke to be in bad taste, but primarily because of my fascination with those red eyes. Night after night I had watched these rabbits and lain abed wondering if they were out there sneering at me, passing snide comments about my lack of hunting instinct. Night after night I had watched the hens shuffle on their perches in the adjoining bedroom and yearned to be out there after those rabbits, the presence of which was torturing me.

At last I could stand it no longer, and urging the whippet and terriers over the wall I cried 'Have at you, you little sods' and was at 'em. Sport? Well I've seen nothing like it, chasing those rabbits by moonlight among the gravestones. 'There he goes whippet, over "Stranger is life than death", dodging past "Here they lie side by side", ducking under "Too soon he went" (which I suppose is a matter of opinion) – Another one there whippet, next to "The angels took him too soon", damn it he's gone, there's a warren under that stone.' By 2.30 a.m. I was exhausted and fell asleep on 'His ways are strange to us' to awake stiff, sore but happy, arriving home just before cock crow which was appropriate considering the denizens of the next bedroom. 'Boy, oh boy, this is really hunting' I thought, and I even had a rabbit to show for my troubles.

So night after night I was in there coursing, and as I got to know the place my haul of rabbits increased. The staff no longer shunned me but now passed comments like desecrator, necrophile and vandal whenever I came into the room. The head had me in twice to warn me of God's (and the Chief Education Officer's) wrath, but I refused to listen, intoxicated by the euphoria of hunting this forbidden land. However, the statement 'All good things must come to an end' is not only a cliché, it is also damnably true, as I was to find out.

The day in question dawned inauspiciously enough when the postman, a kindly soul, very tolerant of my eccentricities, pushed a long-awaited letter into one of the nest boxes in the next bedroom. I leaped up and opened it. A few weeks previous I had seen an article about a man who believed that it was possible for the human race to live exclusively on the petals of a flower called *Tagetes Minuta* (a type of marigold), and to prove it he intended to live for a year on this diet alone. Sensing a kindred lunatic I wrote to him, hoping and praying he was right and I'd be able to say 'sod off' to the head and sow my allotment full of *Tagetes Minuta* and live a life of Riley on marigolds and graveyard rabbits. Sadly, the letter read 'Thank you for your interest in my father's work – unfortunately he has died.' Ah well, you can't win them all I suppose, so I scrapped the marigold plan and caught the bus to school, elated by the fact that tonight, once again, I would be out there after those rabbits.

It was a cold November night with a slight stinging drizzle, the sort of night made for roasting chestnuts around the fire rather than making a sortie into the graveyard. The shed was also cold and I resolved that once I had enough money I'd get a few more hens which would not only give an extra egg or so but also warm the place up a little. Knowing I needed the money to visit Doncaster market and make my purchases there, I resolved, unsporting as it may appear, to block the warren under 'The angels took him too soon' and sell my surplus bunnies at a pub called The Plumpers' Arms. However one should not only not count one's chickens before they're bought at Doncaster market, but also not predict the number of rabbits one is going to catch, and things weren't destined to go too well on this particular night.

Over the wall and at 'em yet once again, and with my mind on one of those Rhode Island Red central heating systems, hunting took on a new and almost frantic urgency. Rabbits abounded that night, racing twixt the gravestones illuminated by the moonlight. 'After 'em whippet' I urged, leaping after the dog past statues of angels and ornate Celtic crosses. She bowled two and triumphantly I planned that if my luck continued we'd add two Khaki Campbell ducks to the central heating system.

We were in an unfamiliar part of the cemetery now, racing between unfamiliar stones bearing unfamiliar epitaphs when suddenly I felt the earth open up under my feet and I fell what felt like a great many feet into an open grave. I lay there stunned for a moment or two in five or six inches of clay slurry watching the asinine face of the whippet staring into the grave. I'd seen situations like this in Lassie films, where Lassie races back and gets help from neighbours by tugging at some kindly old lady's apron, and dragging her to the victim of a fall. I closed my eyes and saw the whippet fetching back the awesome Mrs Buckmoor spade in hand and the old vixen gleefully filling in the grave more in the manner of a Hammer Film production than one of those tear-jerking Lassie epics. The whippet turned her head slightly and looked mystified about the whole crazy affair. 'Ah well,' I mused, 'I can't lie here all night', and raised myself up out of the icy slurry, or at least I tried to. A sudden sharp pain shot up my leg numbing my feet and toes. My ankle was broken. I looked up in dismay only to see the whippet dancing happily around the edge of the grave barking merrily and wagging her tail.

I stood up on one leg looking rather like a clay-covered stork and tried to crawl out of the grave, scrabbling upwards tearing at the earth, but each time I slipped back into the icy slurry. At last I could stand it no longer and panic replaced fear and pain, 'Help' I screamed, now totally heedless of who might come to my aid, but the sight of a flashing blue-and-white light on the skyline quickly restored my sanity. A panda car – and I threw myself flat in the slurry to escape detection. I heard the crunch of feet on frosty ground, saw the flicker of a torch light, heard a car engine starting up again and then silence. I scraped the mud from the face of my luminous watch and noted it was 2.55 a.m. It was 8.10 a.m. before I managed to clamber up the sides of the grave to the surface. A passing newspaper boy, taking a short-cut through the cemetery, bag on back, whistling happily, glanced across at my clay-caked body emerging from the grave. 'Bloody hell' he shouted, throwing his bag down and racing off to the gates. I crawled home, asked Malcolm to phone for an ambulance and in an hour I was in hospital telling lies about the way the accident happened and having my ankle set.

So it came to pass that eventually I did get out of that school and headed south to Lichfield, and my adventure regarding the grave was forgotten, lost as it was among several other lunatic escapades most of which would have qualified me for a test-run in a strait-jacket. Well, the time came when I had reason to return north again for that somewhat abortive interview concerning Richard Whitely and the ferret on *Calendar, Tuesday*. Joe (my co-driver) and I stopped at the studio and were greeted by a porter who raced over to me joyfully saying that he'd read all my books (which wouldn't have been all that difficult as at that time I'd only written one). We got on famously the porter and I, and in no time flat we were on to the times spent up north. I mentioned the district where I lived and the young chap blanched. 'Don't talk to me about that place' he thundered. 'When I was a paper boy in Kimberworth I saw a body climb out of a bloody grave there. Gave me a bloody stammer for years it did, interfered with my education and Mam took me to a psychiatrist because nobody believed me.' Jesus I'll never forget that day he stuttered. I watched him trundle off down the corridor still mumbling to himself. I never told him of course, but if he still reads my books – well, who knows!

—4—

Family Failings

HAVE YOU EVER PLAYED one of those word association games? – If you can call them games that is. You know the sort of thing, the games one plays, heart in mouth, with psychiatrists who are themselves totally bats, knowing that one slip or an irregular answer qualifies a body for at least a 'look see' at a funny farm. Sure as eggs is eggs I'd get cat/dog – or is it mouse – correct, and I might even hazard a guess at black/white. However bear/prison cell would certainly get 'em guessing and probably casting wistful glances at one of those button-up-behind denim jackets with cross-over sleeves, but bear/prison cell it is I'm afraid and I can never look at one of those Warwick emblems of a bear, tied a little too tightly for RSPCA regulations to a ragged staff, without thinking of a night I spent in a Birmingham nick because of a bear – or to be more precise because of events concerning a bear, if one wants to be totally accurate and a bit pedantic.

Dispense with the notion I have a thing about bears, a mild fixation or even a casual interest, because I don't, though come to think of it, mankind has had some fairly barbarous whacks at the *genus Ursidai* which in layman's terms means bears in general. Neanderthal man, semi-apelike creatures, ponderous brutes, with little or no semblance of real human feelings (I had a class full of these at one time), apparently worshipped an oversized brute called the cave bear, a whopper maybe twice the bulk of a good-sized grizzly, rearing it from a cub to maturity, treating it with tender loving care as befitted a god and finally ceremonially whacking it to death with stones and clubs. Still it takes all sorts I suppose, and the poor old cave bear must have breathed a sigh of relief when Neanderthal man finally decided to become extinct – except that the cave bear too had shuffled off its mortal coil when both Neanderthal man, and his outsized pet/victim became the prey of a far more ferocious predator, namely ourselves.

Man's history seems to be intertwined with bears. The Apaches, before the cavalry decided to threaten them too with extinction, believed that a few million years ago a god came to earth and mated with a bear (whatever turns you on I suppose) and produced the first Apache. However for the absolute tops in crazy behaviour regarding bears, and for all things ursine look no further than the customs of the Hairy Ainu, a somewhat peculiar tribe of hunters who live in the northern regions of Japan. The Ainu kill a bear, skin it, butcher its carcass, removing and eating all parts they consider to be even vaguely edible, and stick the bear's head, eyes propped open, on a long pole. They then perform an elaborate and in the light of what is to follow somewhat pointless ceremony apologising to the bear for killing it (a bit late if you ask me) and ceremony over, they promptly pop out and kill another bear.

For big-time bear whacking though, no one and I mean no one, could hold a candle to the Romans, particularly the emperor Gordian I who could justly be considered to have a thing about bears. During the time of the Roman Empire, when the average man in the street behaved like an average Manchester United supporter, the emperors stopped riot and civil strife by distributing free bread and providing bloody and macabre spectacles of men fighting wild animals, and gladiators hacking each other to pieces. A favourite spectacle was to drug leopards, lions, tigers and elephants to a state of frenzy and release the whole demented band into the arena where they fought until only the elephants were left standing. To the victor the spoils – well, not in the arena, for immediately the elephants had stamped the life out of the last tiger or so a host of archers appeared in the wings and peppered the elephants.

Bears were not spared the misery of death in the arena, but it takes a very special sort of bear to come out of a dark cage into a sunlit arena surrounded by a screaming mob and to set about a Christian or two. In fact the majority of brown bears weren't up to it, and even when starved to a state of frenzied hunger, they simply curled up in the darkest corner of the arena and hid from the tumult. The Romans however were an inventive race, and didn't give up easily either. Animal trainers called *bestiarii*, employed by the emperors, devised ingenious ways to allow *Ursus Arctos* to give of his best. A bear would be reared from a cub, and, as bears are slightly more carnivorous than herbivorous, and as there was always a surfeit of spare bits and pieces of gladiators in the arena, it doesn't take much imagination to guess what the bears' main course was. After a while the bear grew to its full stature, a creature damn nigh as large as a bullock, with absolutely no fear of man, and was allowed to kill a young child whose hands were probably broken to prevent damage to the bear. Thus blooded, the bear proceeded up the ratings, demolishing youths, women and finally lightly-armed and untrained men. When the bear was deemed ready for its debut in the arena, it was introduced into the cages of several wild bears who were not only terrified, but starved to induce a very fractious temper, and the bunch was turned loose in the arena. The wild bears went into the crouch in the darkest areas of the amphitheatre, but the tame bears set about their victims with both gusto and relish thereby inspiring the skulkers in the corner into thinking that the arena wasn't such a bad place after all and encouraging them to pitch in while the party was picking up so to speak. Gordian, a particularly enthusiastic bear-destroyer, once staged a spectacle where twenty thousand slaves and convicts fought it out with a thousand bears and archers peppered the winners.

One bear act became a real show-stopper in the arena and quite by accident at that. During the reign of the Emperor Commodus (played by Christopher Plummer – no relation – in the film) a bear trainer performed twixt gladiatorial bouts a dancing bear act, followed by a poetry recital. Commodus, who incidentally often dressed in women's clothes and leaped down into the arena to fight with the gladiators, was seemingly incapable of going more than twenty minutes without a spot of bloodletting, and began to fall asleep when the poetry recital began. He perked up a little when the bear, aroused by the smell of blood from the act previous and upset by the cat-calls of the mob, decided to liven up the act by biting off its trainer's head during the best bit of the iambic pentameter, a gesture which almost brought the house down with applause, and the bear covered in garlands from the delighted crowd was led out of the arena. Still, that's show biz I guess – you get the laughs how you can when you can.

Bears were fairly common in Italy at that time, I suppose – not common enough to become a nuisance to horse breeders, for bears are rough on young foals as I'll explain later – but the natives were reluctant to allow the animal trainers to snatch up all the bears for the circuses. Bears were useful creatures to the Italians, the skins provided rugs, bed coverings, shoes and winter furs and the meat was prized as a delicacy. However here the bear had the last laugh, if laugh you can call it, as bear meat, like the meat of the wild pig, is a rich source of trichinosis, a highly infectious and deadly little roundworm which causes a fatal form of enteritis, which probably saw off a host of Italian and Roman bear hunters – and serves 'em right say I.

Whether or not the animal catchers employed by the Roman circuses saw off the British bear is questionable, for there is no mention of the bear in post Roman/British history though curiously enough the name Arthur, of the Round Table and Excalibur fame, is derived from the Celtic word *Arnth*, meaning bear. One thing is certain; Hywel Dda (which means 'Howell the Good' in English) who drew up an enormous list of the values of sundry items from live cats to marten skins, makes no mention at all of the bear, its skin, its skull or its grease (which incidentally was the principal component of the numerous magical potions used for a variety of purposes ranging from the cure of gout to the creation of a one hundred per cent Hammer Horror Film type werewolf), so we can assume that the bear had become extinct in Britain long before the tenth century.

My bet is the Celts, rather than the Romans, saw off poor old *Ursus Arctos*. The Celts were well known to the Romans not only as breeders of huge hounds which fought in battles twixt beasts and men in the arenas, but also as breeders of first-class horses. Bears are incredibly destructive with horse foals, not because the bear is a natural hunter of horses but simply because newborn foals are curious little creatures without a brain in their elegant heads. Hence the sight of a bear sniffling at a wasp's nest or digging up bluebell bulbs would have prompted the foal to whip over and investigate. After repeated nosings from the foal, even the most patient of bears would have chanced a swipe or so at the young horse and a swipe from a bear leaves a foal in a pretty bad way, if not with a broken neck. Bears are reluctant to leave any meat to waste and would promptly wolf down the foal, hooves, bones, hide and all, so it seems unlikely that the Celts could or would tolerate the presence of such a beast in horse-breeding country; and so the British brown bear went the way of the bison and the mammoth I'm afraid.

Bear-trained acts involving dancing bears, tumbling bears, wrestling bears and even mathematically orientated bears supposed to be able to count to ten by their owners and trainers were fairly common in the courts of certain Saxon Kings, but these bears were certainly not British brown bears. Most of the trainers were Armenians who travelled around Europe with their bears performing at any court or inn where they could earn a few pence, and certainly the skills learned by these Armenian bear trainers were picked up by the gypsy bands who passed through Armenia four hundred years later.

However the British are a vigorous race and dancing bears were unlikely to entertain the typical British man in the street for long. By the 1300s bull-baiting had become the rage, with savage dogs 'sicked' on by even more savage owners, making havoc on some wretched old bull who had outgrown its usefulness as a breeding beast. Quick as a flash some bright spark realised that whereas a bull falling amongst its entrails and wallowing in copious amounts of blood among packs of stunned disembowelled bulldogs was OK as things went, the bear with its claws, teeth and predatory disposition was the real fun creature, and with careful diet, rested up occasionally and wounds treated with hot irons and tar, a bear could be a whole load of fun for several years providing the lunatic fringe didn't insist on evening performances as well as matinées. When one thinks of it, the English are first and foremost amongst the nations of the world in bringing in legislation to prevent cruelty to animals, but only because the British must be the most damnably cruel race on the face of the earth.

Bear-baiting was an awful business which would have sickened anyone with any sense of decency and come to think of it the bears probably didn't appreciate it all that much either. Royalty, and even Will Shakespeare, were really into bear-baiting and revelled in an evening's bloodletting at the bear gardens. Popular fiction states that the bears, which incidentally were chained with a short leash to a pole, were blinded before a battle, to allow the dogs which were being encouraged to fight him a sporting chance, but there is no real evidence to support this theory though in all probability after a few really savage encounters with the bulldogs or mastiffs used in this sport (if sport is the right word) most bears would have lost not only an eye or so but most of their genitalia, and would have been a little short on ears as well.

A 'course', which is the name used for this nasty and bloody spectacle, consisted of setting four or even six mastiffs on a bear simultaneously. The first two or three which leaped at a bear were odds on favourites for coming unstuck, but after these a series of fresh dogs would have wreaked havoc on the poor bear until he collapsed and was declared beaten. It says much for the tenacity of the brown bear that bears were rarely killed during these baits, and, within two or three weeks, they were up and at their adversaries again, chopping, ripping, rending, and breaking asunder as good as new. During the time the bear was recovering the mob usually had to make do with a horse-and-ape-bait – which consisted of a terrified monkey seated on an elderly, but equally terrified horse being dismembered by bulldogs – poor stuff when compared to a real McCoy bear-bait, though the mob were quite easy to please and enjoyed a terrified old sow being slashed, mutilated and killed by mastiffs as much as anything.

Henry VIII, an unpleasant brute even by the standards of the day, was heavily committed to bear-baiting and not exactly averse to any form of brutality and torture for that matter. Henry had so many mastiffs, bulls, bears and other creatures he considered suitable for hunting and torturing, that he made the mastership of these creatures a court office and in 1526 sponsored the building of the infamous Paris Gardens, a horrid place where story has it, long after the building was torn down, the area echoed with the ghastly screams and plaintive moans of stricken animals. Henry had just a spot of trouble about building the Paris Gardens' bear pit and was forced to construct this house of horror at Southwalk, outside the jurisdiction of London, as the Puritans of that city objected to a bear garden; not because of the ferocious cruelty perpetrated there, but simply because the baits were staged on Sundays. Southwalk later became famous for theatres and these tended to put the nose of the owner of the bear gardens out just a little; so the powers that were, being an uncultured bunch of louts decided to close the theatres on Thursdays, to give the bloodletters of the Paris Gardens a chance to regain the public's interest in atrocity and the barbaric torture of bulls, bears and whatever other unfortunate beast was at hand.

So popular was bear torturing that two theatre managers, Henslowe and the actor/manager Alleyn, spent a great deal of their time not treading the boards as the saying goes, but arranging nasty little exhibitions between dogs and bulls, bears and dogs, and just a spot of dog fighting when public interest looked like flagging. Will Shakespeare, for all his love sonnets and delicate turn of phrase, was an ardent fan of the Paris Gardens, or 'Hope Theatre' as the place became known after the Paris Gardens became so offensive to the nose that even the Tudors and Stuarts decided that the hovel had to be replaced. Indeed Will wasn't in any way averse to a spot of top-grade animal torture, and mingled with the thieves, cut-throats, louts and sadists, rubbing shoulders with the seediest members of society as bears pounded dogs to pulp. Two of the bears fought at the Hope Theatre and Paris Gardens, Old Hunks and Sackerson, were so well known by the public, that Will, who hadn't a clue his style of writing would outlast the century, wrote the brutes into his plays.

Sackerson was a fearsome monster by all accounts, a fiend weighing nearly half a ton perhaps, with claws as thick as a man's finger. Repeated torment by dogs, the onslaughts of which were swatted as a man swats a fly, had made the brute doubly dangerous, and transporting such a bear from one pit to another would have taxed anyone's strength and courage. Bears don't exactly hug a man to death, as legends say, but simply hold a man in position to bite him, and it is the bite that kills, taking off the side of the victim's head, flesh and skull to boot. Even the holding grip is usually enough to push in a man's ribs. How Sackerson ended his days is questionable: perhaps he became old, truculent and too fractious to keep, perhaps he died after an incredibly hard and ferocious baiting session. The chances are that he sickened and pined away, his misery at being captive, chained by the neck to a wall, made more so by the frequent rippings and tearings at his flesh by bulldogs and mastiffs. For sheer cruelty the English really take some beating!

Mind you the Spanish run us a close second. Spain is still famous for its bullfights, where incredibly insane young bucks make almost as much money as a British snooker player, simply by allowing a bull to rush at them and slaying it with a sword as it, with luck, flashes past them. Originally bullfighting was performed by a mounted lancer killing a bull, but after the Napoleonic Wars the toreador dismounted and took his chance on foot. The majority of hunters, lurchermen, terrier enthusiasts and shooting buffs have at some time or other had a brush with a bull, usually an overweight Friesian giant, or a gentle white-faced Hereford, the first bred to produce milking cows, the second to produce beef. The Spanish fighting bull is another matter, a totally different kettle of fish in fact. The cows produce only slightly more milk than a goat and the beef is so stringy and tough that only Spanish beggars seem to relish it. In short Spanish fighting bulls were not bred to gratify man's table needs, but simply to satiate his insane desires to watch two beasts slog it out with each other until one or the other died, preferably in a pool of gore. For centuries only the most fierce and courageous bulls were used for breeding, bulls which had shown such phenomenal courage that they were considered too good to be subject to the roars of 'Olé, Olé' and a sharp short stab behind the ears. Sometimes a bull which had shown fantastic courage in the blood and sand spectacle was reprieved and put up for breeding, but only the most ferocious bulls, the gamest, the most dangerous were used for breeding, and over the years a breed far removed from the gentle milk cows evolved until a black devil incarnate was produced, fearing little and heedless of pain.

Men were not the only foes the Spanish fighting bull faced. Now and again the mob thrilled to the sight of two bulls battling it out to the death, but really spectacular contests were staged during the seventeenth and eighteenth centuries. Rich rulers, with more money than sense, brought in a variety of animals to match with their bulls, animals ranging from South American jaguars, African leopards and North African lions to Bengal tigers. Cats are not as courageous as one might imagine, and most are reluctant to make a fight of it with any creature not required for food (perhaps this is an indication of feline intelligence). A fighting bull, one suitably psyched up (and it takes remarkably little to psyche up a fighting bull) simply took the battle to these poor wretched felines, and in no time flat they were fighting for their lives against half a ton of horned ferocity which didn't know the meaning of fear. Jaguars and leopards which can quite easily kill a milk cow, were tossed around like rag dolls and finally stamped to death, and frankly the larger lions and tigers didn't do a whole lot better. It was only when the Spanish started settling in America that they found a suitable match for a first-class fighting bull.

America has always gone in for the oversized; extra large buildings, over-big bridges and even their incidence of violent crime tops that of Europe. The European brown bear is a bulky, powerful customer but he is small fry when compared to his American cousin the grizzly, a gigantic brute nearly as big as a cave bear and sometimes topping eleven feet tall when a large one can be pursuaded to stand upright. Comanche warriors were considered heroes if they could run in and deal such a beast a death blow with a stone knife, which I suppose goes a long way to explain why the Comanches are not only a minority group bordering on extinction but judging from their little hobbies suitable candidates for mental treatment. The grizzly was the ideal opponent for the best strains of Spanish fighting bulls.

To run in on an eight-feet-tall brute (Mexican bears are smaller than the eleven-feet-high Alaskan types) with a stone knife requires not only a person with a somewhat questionable mental health, but a great deal of skill; by comparison to capture a bear by dint of a lariat, or to be precise two or three lariats is almost child's play, though if things went wrong the roper was to use a good old Jewish expression 'really in the sturp'. A bear would be sighted some distance from a town, and a band of Spanish conquistadors (literally, a band of Spaniards who had slaughtered nearly all the native Mexican Indians and stolen their land) set out to hunt it. The bear would be lassooed by one of the cavaliers and would immediately rush the horseman who had roped it. Immediately another cavalier would rush in and also lassoo the bear and maybe a third would also put a rope around the captive beast just for good measure. The bear would then be dragged, tumbled, rolled and pulled to the nearest town – often two or more days journey – and rested up a while. When the bear had recovered from its rough treatment it was pitted against – yes, you've guessed it – a Spanish fighting bull, and if the bull had its own way against leopards, jaguars, lions and tigers, against a bear, well, it was a fairly even match. Most bears were killed by the first rush of the bull and hooked, gored and trampled in minutes, but some learned how to deal with bulls fairly quickly. A bear called General Scott saw off nearly fifty bulls before it had an off-day and went the way of all flesh, trichonosis and all!

Back to Britain once more. In 1835 an act preventing bull- and bear-baiting was passed which effectively outlawed having a whack at any baitable beast, though bear-baiting had long since ceased to be popular – not for any humanitarian reasons, but simply because of the fact that bears were getting a bit scarce in Europe and the cost of bringing them into Britain was a shade prohibitive. True, for a while bears did make the Channel crossing even after 1835 but these were dancing bears trained to jig up and down to the beat of a tambourine, rather than ferocious old warriers like Sackerson or Old Hunks, but even dancing bears didn't exactly live a life of Riley, not by any standards, and their training just about topped it all in the cruelty stakes.

The way circus animals were trained never really attracted attention from the general public. Folk naturally assumed gypsies and other 'canny' folk had some magical power over animals, a sort of King Solomon's Ring magic which persuaded a variety of beasts including pigs, bears and even porcupines into doing an amazing number of tricks. Jack London of *White Fang* and *Call of the Wild* fame actually exposed the whole messy business for the brutal trade it was, and boy oh boy, when London took the lid off the circus business, the world began to realise that many circus beasts weren't trained by kindness and didn't simply perform in public for the hell of it.

Stories of how London chanced on discovering how circus animals were trained are legion and varied. One tale states that one day London visited a state fair which boasted a variety of freaks (popular acts in America during the 1890s, so popular in fact that talent scouts were sent to various institutions freak-spotting) but also a team of Cincinatti dancing geese, geese which were driven on to a metal sheet and jigged around to music – no big show-stopper admittedly, but I suppose the kids liked it. London however, pushed forward and slowly put his hands on the sheet of metal on which the geese were dancing. He moved his hands away fairly sharply by all accounts, for the proprietor of this emporium of horror had lit a kerosene burner under the sheet and the geese jogged around to prevent the delicate membranes of their feet getting roasted.

From that time onwards it was gloves off as far as London was concerned and he turned up other unpleasant little facts during his investigations. In the 1860s a group of Hungarian gypsies called Ursari (from *Ursus* – a bear) visited Europe and America with their dancing beasts. London found such beasts were not trained by gypsy magic and kindness but as cubs were forced to step on heated iron plates to the beat of a tambourine. Later, all a Romany had to do was to produce a tambourine to find Bruin dancing about like Milton Berle threatened with violence. Societies called Jack London Clubs appeared all over Britain and America to stop this type of animal training, and slowly such clubs gained public credibility until circuses were subject to scrutiny from societies preventing cruelty to animals. However to return to bears, or more particularly a particular bear and a spot of investigation into the genealogy of the Clan Plummer.

Now it may come as rather a surprise to know that amongst our clan I am considered as rather an ordinary sort of person, in no way different or peculiar, though come to think of it you'd be hard pressed to find a stranger bunch than the Plummers and related minions. Uncle Billy, a cockfighter, reprobate and womaniser who in the immortal words of one Samuel Clysby, a failed rabbi and herring specialist, 'had women as fast as they could push 'em under him', was considered very unpleasant by Mam, not that her cousins were anything to go by mind you, for you'd have to look around quite a bit to find a bigger pack of nutters anywhere. Take for instance, her cousin Norman who had mental treatment because he had delusions and thought he was a hen. He'd believed this for years and Dad said the only reason Auntie Kim didn't have him treated was because the family needed the eggs. He had a brother Rupert, whose only claim to fame was that he claimed that just before the Somme offensive, a medical officer of some note had by devious unpleasant means extracted the longest tapeworm in the world from Rupert – personally I wouldn't have boasted about this, but then it wouldn't do for everyone to be the same would it. Because of the disgusting parasitic monstrosity, which Rupert had kindly donated to science (and who else would want it), Rupert had been spared the horrors of the first Somme offensive and lay abed while various members of the various medical corps whipped up his bed sheets and shone electric lights up certain parts the nature of which should be best kept to oneself. An embarrassing experience perhaps, but as Rupert explained 'better up the bottom than over the top'. Rupert was a born troublemaker, agin most things, and once received a savage beating from a band of Quakers for explaining his own particular brand of agnosticism by stating that God is so mystifying that for all we know his real name could be Reg Perks – a philosophy which I've never really understood; and his dying words 'Nothing looks worse than the sight of dead nuns in number' has caused considerable interest among the esoteric groups of weirdo philosophers, none of which have the slightest notion as to what the old nutter meant.

I was in school with Rupert's son Percy, a right weirdo by any standards who did unpleasant things with oranges, really unpleasant things believe me and if it hadn't been for the food rationing he'd have done himself a permanent mischief. Percy was quite an academic by all accounts, finishing up in art school, whence he was expelled for making obscene gestures, rolling on the floor, shouting filthy words and generally getting himself well and truly steamed up when the art teacher brought the model in. The college principal slung him out on his ear immediately, after all it isn't natural to get that excited over the sight of a bowl of fruit. Percy was twenty-eight years younger than his sister so his peculiar ways could be attributed to the fact that he was born late in his mother's life. Mind you, his sister wasn't all that normal. Sally had a reputation for being something of a witch – a prophet, a seer, call her what you will – though she knew far more about American soldiers than she knew about the occult. Her credibility came under fire when her prophecy that World War II would end in 1957 didn't quite work out, though judging from her antics with our American allies, her prediction could be regarded as wishful thinking rather than prophecy, if you ask me. She also predicted that in 1971 the world would experience its first extra terrestrial invasion and if it had happened as planned and her rheumatics hadn't have been playing her up she'd have had it off with one of the space invaders no doubt – a curious woman, Sally.

Dad's cousin, Harold Tutt, was another of those characters considered far from normal by the man in the street. Harold's wife upped and left him after Harold in a fit of pique at his wife's unfaithfulness killed her corgi and served it up for Sunday dinner. Harold boasted of his heinous deed repeatedly: 'Make the punishment fit the crime mate that's what I say' he'd storm, which left one thinking who or what in hell his wife had had her fling with. Curious dietary habits seemed to run in the Tutt family. His son Peter, a spotty, unlovely child was sent to private school after mum, incensed by Harold's canine cuisine upped and left the house. Peter was unhappy in private school, and some time during his sixth form he mixed jalap (a violent purgative) with the school custard and laid the entire school low with a bout of stomach cramp which will always be remembered. Peter was expelled and promptly obtained a commission in the army, returning home decorated because he reputedly killed ten men while serving in Korea. Considering Peter was serving in the Catering Corps it makes one wonder how he managed to kill ten men, and whether or not the ten men were on the side of the enemy.

For one hundred per cent lunatics however, strange even by our family's standard, you'd be struggling to better Clive, Dad's cousin's boy, a real one hundred per cent, twenty-four carat gold lunatic. I grew up with Clive who, because he was not only brighter, but also more articulate and better looking than I am, overshadowed me quite a bit and gave me one hell of an inferiority complex, finally treating me as a whipping boy, a butt for his ridiculous practical jokes, and someone to torture, hurt and make unhappy whenever he decided he needed cheering up a little. When I was fifteen I really hated Clive, partly because when we were in public he'd seek out the biggest most violent boy in the room and run over and not only tell him that I'd said he was a homosexual but also mention that I had said I intended to beat the boy up as soon as I got him outside. The result was not only predictable but bloody and unpleasant believe me and I began to hate Clive and his notions of what constituted fun.

I am not against practical jokes, in fact I have something of a jaded sense of humour myself, but cousin Clive took it just a bit far. I took the mouse-trap device in the sweet bag prank with a good grace and I even tried to laugh off having my one and only pair of shoes filled with liquid cow muck when I was paddling out after trout in the nearby brook. I must admit I didn't go great guns on the anonymous phone calls to the police tipping them off that I was guilty of every crime in the district from dope peddling to prostitution, nor were my parents all that happy about the hearse sent to the house every month or so to collect my cadaver, but that was Clive I guess, and for a while I had to grin and bear it.

I left home at sixteen and never went home again until after Mam's death, but somehow or other I kept in touch with some of my cousins, though the term 'in touch' was a decidedly chancy state considering Clive's ability to manipulate electric batteries etc. For all his lunacy he was a real academic – which was another reason to hate him – and finally qualified as a doctor, though for some reason, probably something to do with the money an intern earns, he never practised but became a rep for a pharmaceutical company, selling drugs and poultices to chemists shops and hospitals. Thus, being denied the pleasures that a one hundred per cent weirdo like Clive might experience being able to ask a woman to take her clothes off under the guise of a medical consultant, he became stranger than ever.

I was twenty-nine when Clive turned up again and I was teaching in a quaint old secondary modern masquerading as a comprehensive, and, just like the school, I was getting nowhere fast. I must be unique among teachers in as much as I've never actually ever been accepted for a post if there has been another applicant at the interview. Well, the day of Clive's phone message, once more I left the nasty little secondary modern school for an interview for a post teaching violently disruptive backward boys at an even nastier secondary modern but with the possibility of getting another £120 a year extra for my pains. It doesn't sound much, £120 a year, but I've always been lumbered with the weirdos wherever I've gone and I felt I should get paid for my troubles now. 'You've a natural talent for the difficult cases', a head would remark sarcastically as if I too had problems, and then fling me into a classroom with a bunch of misfits which probably gave Desmond Morris the necessary data for one or two of the nastier chapters in *The Human Zoo*. There's no future in the teaching profession being good with the strange and the disruptive believe me, and after a while a teacher who spends much of his life with such kids becomes as odd as the kids – a little more literate perhaps but equally odd. So once more unto the breach dear friends and yet another unsuccessful interview to depress me still further. I was elated by the fact that the post called for someone interested in pastoral work, but once again my gloom descended when I realised pastoral meant nothing to do with sheep, cows or other livestock – a pity I'm better with these than I am with kids.

I borrowed a suit from a chap called Henry Jaffrey, a rather tyrannical science teacher known unaffectionately as 'stick arse' by the well-thrashed kids, and started out for the school to face the ordeal of an interview, becoming more and more aware that either Jaffrey or I had some awful deformity, for the sleeve of his suit came down just past my elbow and no further. Well, to the school and into the waiting room where the two other applicants sat waiting. The first was a somewhat seedy ex-vicar, aged maybe fifty, whom I suspected had been unfrocked for some nasty little habit or other, as he had that decidedly furtive appearance one associates with discredited clergymen, and had a way of looking at anyone over the top of his glasses which would have merited more than a taste of a knuckle sandwich from the more aggressive of the lower streams of fifth forms I've taught. The second applicant was an ultra-nervous thirty-year-old with a degree in Chinese Fine Art (priceless for teaching backward kids I've always thought), a pronounced tic of the Edgar Allen Poe variety and a tendency to discharge a trickle of drivel from his mouth when he spoke – rather like a soda syphon would best describe the spray. I felt amost confident of my chances of getting the job, really elated, and noticed that for some curious reason my jacket sleeve didn't seem quite as short as it had twenty minutes previous. We chatted a while inanely about nothing in particular in order to get to dislike each other well and truly, while I tried to get down wind of the sprayer whose salivary products resembled Dunnet Bay during a bad gale, and in next to no time it was my turn to face the interviewers.

A quick word about teaching interviewers. An appointment for a post has no relationship to one's ability to do the job in question, but is merely an indication that one is able to run the baffling gauntlet of a hundred odd, bewildering and totally unrelated questions thrown to one by a group who are totally out of touch with reality and classroom problems. No, it's not sour grapes – I'm a lousy teacher and I admit it, but so peculiar, enigmatic and weird are most of the questions, that anyone who can answer these amazing conundrums asked by the typical interviewers could at the next round of celestial elections successfully run for the post of God. Compared to the grim-faced crowd which faced me on this particular day, my family, even poor old Percy, seemed relatively normal. All three interviewers – two men and a third person whom I believed to be a woman but couldn't be certain – sat there grim-faced as if prepared to put on the black cap if I failed to answer their questions correctly. I smiled, they didn't and the conflict began.

'Pies' an elderly near-to-retiring education officer spat out, and stared hard at me as he silently mumbled the word again. 'Pies' he reiterated, and before I had time to explain that I'd eaten he began to elaborate on his riddle which would have not only thrown Oedipus but set the Sphinx back on her hunkers as well. 'Physical, Intellectual, Eduational and Social. How do you reconcile these needs with the nature of your appointment? – Should,' he sneered malevolently, 'we decide to appoint you of course.' 'Well,' I spluttered, feeling a little like one of these primitives from the planet Mongo facing Flash Gordon who was armed with a laser gun. 'Well,' I stuttered, stalling for time, running my hands down the legs of the chair as if to feel for an ejector seat button. 'Well,' I whispered, my mouth dry, my knees knocking and wishing I could come up with a sudden fit of vomiting to break the tension and change the question, but my torturer wasn't having any. 'Pies' the lunatic was reiterating yet once again, but it was no good, I was hopelessly thrown and left the room my head bowed in shame while the next contestant entered the lists wading through the pools of spittle made by the third. The driveller got the job – I believe he lost it a year later when one of his class, infuriated by the youth's constantly shrinking shirts, jumped up and bit him, but that's just me being spiteful I suppose. Anyway I didn't get the job and returned to school my confidence shaken and my jacket sleeve now seemingly up well past the elbow.

I sat with my class towards the end of the afternoon and began to contemplate my future with the assembled oddities (both staff and pupils) contained in the school. Activity-wise it was a quiet afternoon, with only an incident concerning one Jackson of a family of well known police attackers having thrust a rusty piece of chicken wire up one nostril and retrieving it down the other to break the monotony. He sat there, a piece of wire dangling from his snout, glaring, daring all and sundry to touch the wire while the class sat back gasping in admiration for a piece of human ingenuity they considered level with the building of the pyramids in the story of man's achievements. 'Why don't we 'ave sex lessons?' chirped up Rosie, a fifteen-year-old who had made a considerable sum of money since she realised boys were different from girls. 'Why can't we 'ave sex lessons, sir?' – she threw in the sir just for good measure, nothing more nothing less. I stifled the desire to shout 'Piss off Rosie, giving sex education lessons to you is like giving Evil Knievel an L-plate. You know more about bloody sailors than the Royal Naval Academy at Dartmouth' but managed only a wry smile as a reply, choked as I was with a sense of inadequacy and failure.

Mrs Cobbler, the school secretary, whose name had caused considerable mirth over the years, popped in to ask how I'd done at the interview, and to mention that my cousin was phoning me at 4.00 p.m. School secretaries are priceless ladies and literally run most secondary modern, comprehensive and grammar schools, for gifted with the ability to sort out educational nonsense from more educational nonsense, they keep a school on a relatively even keel. 'Well,' she said consolingly, on hearing of my defeat at the hands of the Pieman, 'you're happy enough here aren't you?'. I glanced around the class bitterly. Harrison had leaped up and was complaining that Tomkins was picking his nose, Harrison's nose, not his own; I choked back my nausea wishing I was some place else – anywhere else to be exact. 'Yes I suppose so', I murmured, and Mrs Cobbler minced off leaving me to cope with the lunatics and to wait for 4.00 p.m., for whatever cousin was intending to phone me.

The phone rang at four o'clock sharp and the cousin turned out to be Clive. After a few 'how's the family' comments he got down to the point of the phone call. 'I've got a bear, Bri, come down and see it.' 'A bare what?' I asked, but he was too excited with his latest acquisition to give much attention to my weak joke, and went on about the bear he had purchased from some zoological supplier. A Himalayan bear, the sort commonly imported during the 1960s and sold to unsuspecting suckers with a yen for something exotic. I'd seen bears like this before and watched sundry exhibitionists who had a yen to have everyone notice them have their properties torn asunder by the beasts, but Clive seemed really excited about his acquisition and as I was the only member of the family batty enough to be interested in bears he had phoned me and invited me down to his London flat to see the brute. 'What the hell,' I thought, 'I've nothing else to do anyway' and decided to pick up the loose change I'd saved in the empty Robinson jam pot and whip down to London to see Clive.

A quick digression at this point. If today one was to walk into a pet shop and order a small unusual predator, for instance a fox, the seller would need to know if the public health people, called the Department of the Environment these days, had granted one a licence to keep the 'critter' and would request a whole load of other papers before parting with the beast. Before 1973 this wasn't the case and if a householder fancied a lion, a puma or considered that every home should have a rhino, he simply saved up the cash and went out and bought one. Lunatics parading in Birmingham with black jaguars on a leash, or council tenants with a lion in the backyard abounded. A couple of days ago two council house tenants in the district where I teach fought a ding-dong battle because a cat belonging to one had killed his neighbour's pigeons; but before 1973, this would have been considered small fry with one irate council house tenant bellowing over the wall at his neighbour: 'You bastard, your crocodile has just ripped a piece out of my ocelot.' But the 1973 Act changed all that, and now one's place has to resemble a rather swish Fort Knox before one is considered for a licence to keep a lion, and to keep a bear in one's flat is really infra dig. Come to think of it when I consider the problems Clive had, keeping a bear in one's flat wasn't such a good idea either before or after the 1973 Act.

It was near Christmas, a bad time to travel to the metropolis, when I counted up my spare cash, rummaged a little through my friend's dustbin for returnable bottles of any kind and bought a ticket to London. Travelling to London at any time is murder, for not only do I find cities a bit claustrophobic, but I also hate travelling on trains, particularly trains full of bright young dolly birds dressed to kill and young bucks who are going places wearing trilby hats, expensive sheepskin coats and all looking the same. My donkey coat donated free of charge but unintentionally by Wimpey (left in my tiny two up and two down by a friendly Irish labourer) began to look even shabbier by the minute. Two soldiers full of the joys of spring boarded the train at Birmingham with fish and chips in the customary paper wrapping. 'Are you sure this fish is cooked properly?' shouted one. 'Why?' replied the other. ''Cos the bastard has just started eating the chips' shouted the first, flashing after a mini-skirted dolly and receiving a quick rebuff from the same. The train was packed to capacity and I hate crowds as well as trains. I sunk into the corner seat opposite a madman who rambled on about having been kidnapped by Venusians for stud purposes. He was an odd looking chap with a long and ever-runny nose and I reflected that either the Venusian women had some pretty odd tastes in stud mates or else the science of genetics was way behind on Venus. In despair I began to think of ways of getting a railway carriage all to myself. I had a girl cousin who was an expert at such tricks. She'd lean out of a railway carriage as it stood in the station shouting 'Come in there's plenty of room, do come in' to passers by. She always had a carriage to herself. If a carriage had just one person seated in it she'd push herself close to the passenger and smile inanely. It worked a treat mate, it worked a treat, but I'm not one of the braver members of the clan believe me. Another way so I'm told is to have a very large, savage looking Dobermann Pinscher – you know, the sort that snuffed out poor old Gregory Peck in *The Boys From Brazil* – and board a train shouting 'For Christ's sake don't stroke him'. That too has the desired effect but I had neither courage nor Dobermann so I sat out the maelstrom of humanity opposite the galactic stud in silence, sinking deeper into my seat by the minute, becoming the very epitome of a shabby nonentity.

London, the buzzing tube stations with homo hurridus going like a bat out of hell, pushing me around while I tried to work out my way to Clive's flat, and at last I found the place, a huge stark complex, like a concrete ant-hill I thought at the time. Two coloured boys were spraying 'Go home honkeys' in the porch of the complex – a hard act to follow I must admit, and when I asked them where Clive lived they gave me a long hard glance. 'You from the ministry Mister? Come to see the nutter about his "thing"?'. The ambiguity of the question took some little time to dawn on me and by that time I was in the lift going up. A psychologist called Baxter is dead agin flats – he's agin most things actually but he believes flats have a disorientating effect on people, making them lose perspective about what goes where. Clearly Baxter was correct for the last occupant of the lift must have been very disorientated as he'd mistaken the place for a toilet. I stood in the dryest corner and watched the badly mutilated lift shoot up to the fourth floor where it stopped and two chaps dressed in Kaftans got in as I got out.

I walked along the corridor and knocked on the door of Room 124 and was aware that a large, seemingly detached eye seemed to be watching me through the peep-hole anti-thief device in the door. There was a rattle of catches and bolts, a jangle of chains and Clive opened the door a shade, peering through the narrow gap at me. A stench like an uncleaned ferret cage hit me smack in the face. 'Come in', he whispered, and pushed me into the room slamming the door behind me. The stench was awful and as I gazed around the flat I realised that the furniture had been ripped to shreds, torn to pieces and hacked asunder, slashed as if a herd of professional vandals had done the place over as one of those community projects which are now so much in vogue at the moment. 'Jesus,' I hissed, 'the sods have burgled you.' Clive gave me a sidelong pitying glance and beckoned me to sit on a gutted easy chair. 'No,' he replied, 'want some tea?' He opened the kitchen door and the beast rolled in like an amorphous ball with teeth and claws. I fell back into the chair, hands gripping its arms in a state of terror. Clive saw my face and tried to calm me. 'He's perfectly tame providing you don't go near his dung corner and touch his shit. He cuts up a bit rough then.' I was about to say that at that moment the very last thing I wanted was a handful of bear faeces, but by this time the thing was towering over me, breathing unpleasant breath into my face and treating me to a flash of teeth which left one in no doubt that bears were carnivorous. I can remember thinking that the crescent of white on the brute's chest looked horribly like a bib and I was just getting round to remembering that one of Jim Bridges' friends had had his ears bitten off by a bear when Clive appeared cup in hand.

I sat there, still petrified with terror, and mentioned the Bridges incident. 'Different sort of bear' munched Clive, treating the brute to a swift kick when it tried to snatch an Eccles cake slice from Clive's mouth, and the creature, suitably chastened, sulkily rolled off to shoot a stream of urine against the bathroom door. I couldn't help thinking about the joke about the man who kept a twenty-eight stone gorilla in his house and was asked by a friend where, as he euphemistically put it, the gorilla 'did its business'. 'Wherever it likes' was the reply. Clearly the bear had a lot in common with the gorilla but it messed and mucked only in certain places as I later discovered when I tried to pass these spots and was savagely attacked by the brute. Clive was dead right about not touching the bear's faeces believe me and the bear guarded them so particularly that it was a wonder that its body ever considered parting with them.

It was a horrid weekend and while I learned quite a lot about Himalayan bears and their kith and kin, I also learned a lot about weirdo relations and made a mental note not to visit Clive again. So it was I sat in the train and travelled north to Rotherham. I changed trains at Birmingham and sat in a compartment by myself, musing over life in general and my deranged cousin in particular. A tweedy lady totally devoid of sex slid into the compartment and sat down next to me taking out her copy of *The Times Educational Supplement* – a magazine for discontented teachers. She glanced across at me, eyed my shabby clothes disdainfully and wrinkled her nose in disgust at my appearance – at least I thought it was at my appearance but at Derby another chap joined us and he too began to sniff and wrinkle his nose. It took sometime for me to understand why for I am, I admit, naturally just a bit pungent; but the stay in Clive's flat, the constant presence of bear faeces (which I was warned not to touch) had permeated my clothes with a rancid musky smell, a smell so strong that even after several trips to the launderette, the kids in school remarked on the pungence. I explained it was a new deodorant called 'Brute'.

I forgot about Clive, his antics and his faeces-fixated bear and had resumed work in Nutters Gulch (as my class were rather unaffectionately known by the other staff) when I saw a newspaper cutting of a bear reaching out of a Jowett Javelin car (dates you a bit, Bri me boy!) and snatching an ice-cream out of some screaming girl's hands. All bears look alike to me and I can't recognise one ursine from another, but the Jowett Javelin looked a bit familiar (a now rare Volkswagen type vehicle as sturdy as a tank and the only vehicle of its kind capable of containing a bear). I shook my head at the incident and drove all thoughts of Clive 'Grizzly' Edwards from my mind, but that afternoon I had another phone call from Clive and had to listen to a heart-rending story of a spot of unrequited love – slightly tinged with a hint of terror if you ask me.

Now to all those who go a searching for all these women, from love-sick swains to degenerate old roués, one piece of advice. If you have a bear in the house and you intend taking some female home for a spot of naughty or even a quiet social chat, for Pete's sake tell her you have a bear before you get in the front door. Clive had met some elegant charmer called Angelique and was so impressed with her that he'd cleaned up his place (which probably caused the price of Dettol's stocks and shares to soar) and even bought new furniture, and thus confident of a spot of evil he invited the girl home where, with customary Edwards aplomb, he raced her through to the bedroom leaving a trail of mixed assorted clothes across the floor of the living room. Clive lost no time making her aware of his intentions and if Clive told the truth Angelique wasn't exactly averse to a spot of naughty herself. However halfway through Act I the 'two's company' sequence became a horrid 'three's a crowd' nightmare as the bear rumbled into the bedroom and tried to get into the act. The inevitable happened with the half-naked Angelique racing down the stairs screaming and Clive, also half-naked, racing down the same stairs trying to pacify her. Two navvies disturbed by the furore popped their heads out of their flats, saw what they considered to be a rape and beat eight bells out of Clive.

Clive however went round to Angelique's flat the next day to apologise, roses in hand, and allowing Angelique just enough time to recover from her Valium-induced daze, he apologised profusely and asked her out to dinner to make it up to her. She must have really fancied Clive for she accepted – and brother, any woman who comes back for seconds after such an experience must really be keen on a chap. So it was they walked down to the car arm in arm with

Angelique willing to forget and forgive. 'Where do you want to sit?' said Clive pointing to the Jowett, 'in the front with me or in the back with him?' He never saw Angelique again – hence the distressed phone call.

Clive asked me to meet him in Birmingham and he seemed so distressed, so at his wit's end that finally I agreed. So that Friday I hitched a series of lifts down from Rotherham to Birmingham meeting Clive at New Street Station. I felt so sorry for the poor devil that I had forgotten that he had a sense of humour which would have appealed only to the Marquis De Sade, but long before the evening was through I was to have cause to remember it, and brother, oh brother, did I have cause to remember. We travelled to a quiet pub in one of the suburbs of Birmingham, a place which catered for iron workers and men who have grown old in the dark satanic mills of heavy industry until all they want to do at night is to sup a few pints, click a few dominoes and play a few hands of cribbage, a baffling game full of fifteen twos and pairs. Clive sat there lamenting his fate and bleating piteously about how Angelique had for some curious reason best known to herself, refused to see him again, and for some equally curious reason a council official and an advisor from the public health had called to deliver a summons insisting that Clive be shot of the bear. For the life of him Clive couldn't see why, and he pointed out to the officials that there was nothing whatsoever in the renting regulations mentioning anything at all specifically about bears in the flat. He whined piteously about how he had been forced to give the bear away to a zoo and how difficult it was to find a zoo which wanted a Himalayan bear, even a 'free to a good home' bear. Oddballs often have difficulty getting rid of unwanted exotic pets as it happens and a tale will illustrate my point. Not that I'm an expert on sewers mind you, but New York has the biggest and the best anywhere. The sort of sewers where Harry Lime could really live it up undetected for years – though perhaps living it up isn't the best term to use concerning living in sewers. Back to New York however. About twelve years ago an electrician was repairing an installation in the sewer when he panicked and dashed to the surface screaming blue murder that a crocodile had attacked him. His fellow workers were about to phone for a doctor from the 'Belle Vue Happy House' for they considered their work-mate was a suitable case for treatment, when one of them noticed the electrician had one hell of a bite in the seat of his pants, the sort of bite which could only have been inflicted by a Great Dane with power driven jaws, or, and now they had to admit it, a crocodile. The team descended into the sewers and shone a beam around the tunnels. Harry Lime would have been awarded a Congressional

Medal of Honour for just staying down there. The place was a regular Aladdin's cave for creepies and biters – particularly biters – a regular palace of varieties of exotic beasts which just shouldn't have been in a New York sewer. Alligators slugged it out with Indian gharial crocodiles while monitor lizards looking like something out of Conan Doyle's *Lost World* flicked out a tongue or so at passing rats. The group beat a hasty retreat and the city officials sent down a research team to investigate how in hell these nightmare beasts finished up in a sewer. Well, some four years previous, it transpired, the pet shops in New York had had a run on exotic critters, totally unsuitable beasts for flat dwellers even when the beasts were young. Once their owners had tired of the cutest little alligator in Fourth Street and the pet-shop owner had sensed the monster was growing a bit too big to be resold and anyway had probably stocked up with a consignment of equally unsuitable racoons, the disenchanted alligator fanatic could do no more with his pet but flush it down the loo and hope for the best. Running the gauntlet of detergents and an amazing variety of what is scientifically and collectively known as 'yucky' the beast began to flourish on the offal, blood, waste and rats in the sewer, and now without further ado back to Clive.

We were about to pack up and go home, Clive to London and me towards the M1 north when a very depressed cribbage player appeared, crib-board in hand and despondency written all over his face – a grey cadaver of man ground down by heavy industry and as it transpired marital problems. He slammed down the crib-board on the table, took out a worn deck of cards and uttered loudly 'I've 'ad enough of 'er, I'm going to pissin' kill me'se'n'. The regulars didn't even bother looking up from their dominoes, but a strange rosy glow had suffused Clive's face, a glow which I'd seen a hundred times during childhood, a glow which had boded ill for a hundred innocent bystanders. The cadaver-faced man elaborated, 'I've 'ad a pissin' 'nough of 'er, a pissin' 'nough, I'm going to pissin' kill meself'. Clive spoke up softly at first, gripping my arm as I tried to get up and hightail it out of the pub before the storm broke. 'A moment sir,' said Clive in his deepest most resonant stage voice, hamming it a bit and sounding a little like a Vincent Price impersonator. 'A moment sir, I could not but help noticing your rather odd desire to shuffle off these mortal coils and wondered if I could be of some assistance to you in your enterprise.' I tugged madly to get away from Clive who was now sounding like Mephistopheles trying to build up his clientèle. There was a click of dominoes and the whole pub tuned into the conversation, and Clive gripping my arm the tighter went into Act II, Scene 2. 'If, sir, you are keen on ending it all I can certainly be of assistance to you, for there are certainly people who would pay very good coin of the realm to watch someone end it all.' A domino poised in mid-air, the lamp light streamed off the six and four, 'A fifteen two and one for a jack' froze on a man's lips, and an atmosphere like something out of Rod Serling's *Twilight Zone* pervaded the room, the silence broken only by a sibilant hiss of ' 'Es pissin' mad' from the would-be traveller to the land from which – well, you know the rest. I tugged madly sensing the outcome as a hound dog senses an oncoming storm. Clive however, who lacks such a sixth sense, and is a bit limited on the other five as well if you ask me, blundered on. 'If, sir,' (Vincent Price again) 'you will give me a few days notice, I can obtain the services of an asbestos barn, and there in the presence of a select group of paying spectators you can sit yourself in a bath of petrol and flash yourself into a screaming but colourful demise.' The victim's mouth dropped open but no words came. 'Should however you wish to end it all immediately,' Clive continued ghoulishly, 'a few select phone calls to suitably rich clientèle and my friend here' (who incidentally was tugging like mad to get away) 'who is a priest travelling incognito, will shrive you instantly and we can finish the evening in a blazing, screaming finale.' After that I'm a bit vague about what happened and all I can recollect is a blur of tables being overturned, domino players running amok, red and whites screaming to a halt and Clive and I spending the night in a none too salubrious cell in a Birmingham Police Station.

I don't know what weekends are like in police custody, but I can vouch for the fact that Fridays are bloody awful. It was seemingly a full house with Clive and I sharing a block with a half-mad Scotsman and a drunken Irishman whose legs were none too steady but who was in first-class voice. The slam of the cell door put the fear of God up me, and the rest of the night will always be there at the back of my most horrible dreams, the silence of the evening being punctuated only with the repetitious screaming of obscenities from the Scotsman and non-stop cacophonous choruses of 'Mother Macrea' from the other madman. All in all, I didn't exactly enjoy the Friday night, and Saturday morning and the prospect of spending the weekend in nick to appear before the magistrates on Monday morning filled me with dread.

Well, morning and a mug of tea: with the Scotsman coming out with a brand new set of blasphemies every few moments, and the Irish gentleman, now with a king-sized hangover, complaining about the noise in the place. Over tea a kindly bobby asked what Clive and I were doing there, and we explained. He sat there in disbelief and fetched another equally fascinated bobby, not quite as kindly as the first maybe, who also heard the tale before fetching a sergeant, who heard Clive out before fetching an inspector. The inspector listened, not so patiently, glancing at his watch every few minutes throughout the tale. Clive finished and took a swig of his now very cold tea. The inspector stood up and addressed us; 'Get out of here you stupid sods and don't come back to this part of Brum again', and with that we found ourselves outside in the cold morning air, Clive heading car-wise and me bumming a lift to the motorway. I never saw Clive after that, and never wanted to either, but do you know I can't help wondering what in hell happened to his bear.

HAGGARD & THE GAME CHICK

—5—

Haggard

SHE CAME IN out of the sun that morning, beating low along my ragged hawthorn hedge, and snatching a 'game fowl' poult with contemptuous ease, despite the frenzied cackling of the hen. I cursed her, stoned her, screamed execration on all her kind, but in my heart of hearts, for the hell of me, I could not stifle the desire to own and train her.

I was in no position to own a sparrow-hawk at that time, nor was I competent to train one. My early attempts at rearing and training these short-winged predators had all ended in disaster, each down-covered chick becoming a filthy emaciated skeleton before tottering and squawking its way to a pitiful death. To rear and train such a bird requires both skill and patience, a patience not usually given to ordinary men and certainly not to me. I am a competent dog trainer, not a great one I admit, but competent enough for my dogs not to disgrace me in public. I was no falconer, however (though falconer is scarcely the correct word to use, for he who sets out to train and fly hawks rather than falcons is called an austringer), yet at each and every opportunity I snapped up offers of hawks, buzzards and kestrels with alacrity.

Once, and only once I trained (though considering the relationship I had with the bird, trained is scarcely the word) a wild caught sparrow-hawk, trapped or netted by a famous Kentish bird-catcher, who was an even more famous Kentish thief. A wild caught bird is called a haggard from the word *hagar*, a Hebrew word meaning wild, as opposed to a nestling which is called an eyass. A haggard requires less entering to quarry than does an eyass, for it has had its foolishness tempered in the fire of experience, and while an eyass starved down to fine condition, a condition known as yarak, will try for any quarry – even venturing a 'putt' at any dog which offends, a haggard has learned discretion, learned which foes are dangerous, which quarry is difficult to take and likely to cause the hawk injury. Still a haggard is certainly more dextrous at taking quarry than a nestling trained to hunt by man. Yet a wild caught bird seldom becomes really tame, never really accepting the partnership of man, dog and hawk. A haggard is always wary of man, always fearful, ever on edge as if waiting for the first opportunity to sever the relationship and return to the wild; but once again I lose the thread of my tale for my story is not meant to be a manual for austringers, a book I will never be competent to write I fear, but simply an account of the days I spent relentlessly pursuing and attempting to train 'my hawk'.

It is curious but even in her chicken-stealing days she was already 'my' hawk and I suppose even before I trapped her we had an affinity with each other, for heaven knows we had much in common. I had arrived in the district where I now live, impoverished, untidy but relatively clean and still possessing a modicum of respectability, but my attempt to opt out of teaching, my stab at what hippies and allied weirdos are wont to call existentialism had taken a devastating toll on my physical and mental health. Most hippies and other eccentrics who choose to drop out of what today is known as the rat race, are fair-weather survivors. During the summer months and into the season of mists and mellow fruitfulness, like grasshoppers they live an idyllic life basking in warmth, mindful that when the first frosts of winter bite, when the first signs of adversity threaten they can return home to scolding daddy who though he will make them cut their hair, relinquish a little of their Bohemian ways, will tend and support them and keep them fit and well to enjoy yet another summer of 'roughing it'. I had no such generous daddy, no such family who would take me in during the difficult patches of my attempt to reject the values of modern society. I had severed connections with my family some fifteen years previous and had not seen them since, knowing as I did that they too breathed a sigh of relief when I walked out of their banal, boring and uneventful lives.

Now, at the age of thirty-one, I realised I had little to show for my time on this planet. In my last year of teaching I had earned £11.54 a week, the sort of money an average wage-earner would spend keeping a large alsatian, and though I placed little value on wealth, I had to admit that not only had I nothing to show for my six years of teaching, but I had also been desperately unhappy in each and every school, the headmaster of which had seen fit to give me glowing references in the fond hope I'd leave and pass on to another school. A sense of failure is the most demoralising of sensations and brings about all forms of maladies from depression to stomach ulcers, but worst of all, it takes away one's self respect and pride. Hence when I opted out of teaching, deciding to live without dole or other means of support, bartering for my necessities, living a hard, rough and demanding life, I was really in no condition physically or worst of all mentally to attempt the leap.

I had spent August frittering away my month-in-hand wages, lolling in the warm summer sun while the rest of the world seemed to slurry along the busy A38, but as soon as my money ran out and leaf fall heralded the coming of a particularly hard winter, I felt a sudden panic and a hopeless sense of inadequacy.

I had been trained as a zoologist, given a brief but rather pointless spell of teacher training and cast out into the world. All in all I was fit for nothing. I had no skills, other than the techniques I had learned as a bricklayer's hod-carrier one back-breaking summer holiday in 1961, and I was ill-equipped to survive the freezing winter which lay ahead of me. Had I sense, I would have set to gathering the piles of deadwood that littered the grove near my house. As it was I let it lie there for the taking whenever I wanted it, but I was ill-trained to cope with the fearful winter that was to follow that warm, wet and almost miasmic autumn.

Winter had come suddenly without warning and one morning I awoke to find that the tarpaulin which covered the shed-like hovel in which I lived had sagged under a great weight of snow. I cleaned the icy rime which coated the inside of my windows and peered out. Lane, hedges, fields were made plains by the snowfall of the night previous and I spent an icy finger-numbing day trying to forage for deadwood under the snow, rummaging like an inefficient reindeer.

I built a fire of sorts, a smouldering, smoke-producing, flameless fire, which gave little heat to my frosted fingers and hands, and lay back in my broken chair to take stock of the situation. On reflection it was a lot worse than I had anticipated. Two feet of snow covered the land and snowploughs never worked the lanes which criss-crossed this sparsely populated district. My fire began to smoulder to nothing and once more I was forced to visit the grove and feel around in the snow for fallen branches. Night came and a crackling sound beneath my bedroom window indicated that the surface of the snow was freezing, and next day I would have to crash through the frozen surface to reach the grove. I viewed the prospect with dismay and never in my life have I felt more depressed and suicidal.

I obtained my water from a tub at that time, a barrel placed beneath the pipe which tapped the gutters of my roof, a mucky, leaf-filled water source, but water nevertheless. That night however the entire barrel turned to ice, ice which pushed upwards out of the barrel in the form of an incongruous plug. I tried melting snow in the kettle, but that too proved an abortive venture for an enormous quantity of snow melts to form a mere drop of water and I achieved nothing except burning the bottom from my kettle.

I have always delighted in the fact my cottage is secluded, but there are times when its very seclusion causes my spirit to plummet to near-suicidal depths. Winters are the worst times, times when I become aware of how inadequate I am and how little I have gained from my useless, pointless existence on this planet. At times like these my manic-depressive pendulum swings to its lowest point and refuses to budge. That winter, cold, beaten by the elements, dispirited and undernourished, I began to question the reason for my existence and to muse on my failure as a person. I had failed at every job I had attempted, been coaxed to move on by headmasters who were all too aware that not only was I a poor teacher, but that I was 'different', and to be 'different' is a cardinal sin in the teaching profession. I can remember one particularly black depression, when gazing through my window at the snow-filled roads, I began to doubt my own sanity. For a moment my spirits lifted as I remembered someone having said that the truly insane are unaware of their predicament and that the fact that one questioned one's own sanity was an indication that one had not toppled from the slender tight-rope of normality. I became oddly and unnaturally cheerful about this until I remembered that the statement regarding one's sanity had been made by Guy de Maupassant, who had finished his days in a lunatic asylum, 'a hopeless, raging' madman.

The post van passed that morning clearing two parallel lines in the snow, bringing a letter from a friend of mine who had remained teaching at that soul-destroying school in Rotherham, unhappy and disillusioned, as are most thinking teachers. He regarded my opting out of teaching with a degree of admiration and eulogised on my freedom, envying me my lot in life. I gazed around my bare unfurnished cottage and wondered what inadvertant lie I had told him to make him imagine that I was living an idyllic existence. In the frosted window I saw my own reflection and was shocked at how ravaged I appeared. I was always the down-at-heel schoolmaster with unpressed trousers, creased shirts and unmatching ties but now I resembled some emaciated Ben Gunn, some sweater-clad Alexander Selkirk.

To relieve my depression I walked, bow-legged, along the tyre tracks cut by the mail van to check my carefully positioned snares, but my success in snaring did little to lift my spirits. Two wires had been pulled tight as if a creature had been ensnared in the wires and had slipped clear of them like a well-oiled Bedouin thief. Another yielded a head of a rabbit, the body of which had been eaten away by a fox or perhaps a feral cat, for half-wild cats abounded in this district at one time. I can remember gazing at the fishy eyes of the rabbit and envying its lot in the shape of things, knowing that at least this rabbit was spared the awful cold of the winter. I picked up the head, pocketed it to feed my ferrets, and waddled home again only to find my neighbour, Mrs Harrison, had also made use of the path cleared by the mail van and had left a large fruit cake on my doorstep.

I ate the offering hurriedly watching the gusts of wind move the loose snow to and fro, and then quite suddenly I looked up and saw her, a female sparrow-hawk, still-hunting, perched on the leeward side of the moss-encrusted oak tree opposite my hovel. She sat there completely motionless, blending into the dark branches, sitting out the freezing day, an opportunist waiting for some luckless sparrow or brainless finch to pass beneath her, rummaging for scraps of still edible seed exposed by the tracks of the mail van. I walked outside to view her more closely and she floated off like some child's kite drifting on the wind. I reflected we had much in common. Her mutes dropped beneath the tree were green, a sure sign that she too was suffering from the rigours of the winter, for avian digestion is unlike that of a mammal and when a bird is forced by hunger to use up its store of body fat, the droppings become a vivid emerald green colour. I can remember watching her float off from her still-hunting perch, her wings slowly rowing across the snow-covered hedges, and feeling a curious affinity for her. Both of us were loners, content – or maybe very discontent – with our own company; both Ishmails rejected by humanity, me for my odd behaviour and her for her predatory ways. She had somehow survived an autumn in the nearby pheasant wood, for there hawks were shot regardless of legislation, their bodies thrown casually under some hedge rather than sported on some gibbet, alongside rats, stoats and other undesirables. At that moment in time I knew we had much in common.

As she beat slowly over the hedgerow I noticed her wing sported a white feather, a freak of nature perhaps or simply the result of an accident which had ripped out a wing feather which had been replaced by a temporary flight of a lighter colour. Whatever the cause of the odd flight feather it was to distinguish her from the rest of the hawks hunting the district and eventually to contribute to her demise.

I saw her most days perched on the branch of the oak and marvelled at her effortless method of hunting. Finches, sparrows and allied passerines flocked to feed on the crumbs and scraps I threw them, and when she deemed the time was right she dropped like a stone among them, snatching up a luckless victim and flapping off to her plucking post on Cope's gate to strip the tiny corpses of their feathers as fastidiously as a cat or an effeminate French gourmet. I felt a vile Judas throwing crumbs to lure in her prey but try as I might I found it difficult to stifle my excitement as I watched her body pulsating with predatory energy preparing to make a lunge at the feeding songsters below the tree. She became aware that this stretch of trees near my cottage was her territory, and although she vanished for a week at a time sometimes, like as not I would wait and peer out of the dirty windows of my cottage and find her fusing into the outline of the trees. The grove, and my acre and a quarter of weed-filled garden became her domain, and later, much later, I was to regret encouraging her to stay.

Winter dragged on and my store of potatoes and swedes, a legacy of the previous tenant of my hovel, began to diminish. My snares were often empty now and I was forced to travel further afield to set them, often on land which was keepered. My clumsy amateur attempts at purloining rabbits were never detected and I congratulated myself on my skill as a poacher. Funnily enough some fifteen years later I learned that the man who keepered the land at that time knew of my poaching but tolerated it as he considered me half-witted or addled-brained and felt sorry for me. So preoccupied was I with staying alive that I forgot about my white-flighted sparrow-hawk until the spring and then alas I had good cause to remember her.

Spring came and the weather staggered and slithered into warmer days, and with the coming of the finer weather my spirits began to revive. Sometime in March the Inland Revenue suddenly began to realise that I was still alive, unemployed, undernourished but still alive and after a curious series of letters which requested to know why I had not collected the dole money which they pointed out in true Welfare State English 'was due to me', decided to recognise my existence and sent me a tax refund for the year I had spent teaching in that nasty little Rotherham school. The sum was a trivial amount, scarcely enough to buy a very large ice-cream, but with money jingling in my pockets I felt elated, glad to be alive, and despite my ragged looking clothes and my cardboard-soled shoes, as rich as Croesus.

Monday came and I walked to Lichfield to mingle with the crowd of would-be purchasers of small livestock in the market. Markets, particularly livestock markets, fascinate me and the sight of a mixed band of people from five-year-olds to geriatrics carrying cardboard boxes filled with anonymous animals and birds about to be auctioned off still gives me a terrific kick, and I felt the £4.50 already beginning to burn a hole in my pocket. I knew that, despite my financial position, despite my state of penury and my low physical condition which would certainly have benefited more from the purchase of a bun than a bird, I would rub shoulders with, the crowd of bidders and buy something. A fascinating array of useless creatures which would certainly impoverish me still further sat there in cages and boxes, rabbits which children had outgrown, ferrets useless now that the summer and the cessation of rabbiting was nigh and a variety of battery fowl, ill-feathered, bewildered and baffled by their new-found but temporary freedom, all waited to go, metaphorically speaking of course, under the hammer.

I finally settled for the purchase of a silky hen, a weird frizzy-feathered gentle soul who resembled a chicken put together during a caprice by Chagal. Even to my inexperienced eye she was a geriatric, well past her prime as a layer, her feathers matted with dirt and dung, a clear indication that she had once been perhaps a beloved child's pet and that the child had grown tired of her. I bought her because she looked wretched, unwanted by anyone. Indeed no one else bid for her and when I raised my hand to the auctioneer's opening suggestion of 10p, I became the owner of one silky hen, aged, and of doubtful purity, together with her Persil carrying box. I bought a tea and a rather dry scone in the nearby Smithfield public house and peeked in at my purchase, offering her a crumb of scone which she pecked up as tamely as a Trafalgar Square pigeon. I felt mildly ridiculous – a grown man who had spent 10p on a tame scruffy hen which was unlikely to lay and would help contribute to my state of penury still further, and as I carried her home walking the three miles to my cottage, I took to wondering why the devil I had bought her.

Silkies are ornamental fowl, bred and designed to look like Pet's Corner poultry rather than to be commercial layers but though even a good Silky would have to be coaxed into laying a hundred eggs a year they are renowned broodies and rearers of chicks. In fact, if I left an egg or two in her orange-box nesting compartment for a day or more, she settled down on the sterile clutch shuffling like a washer woman and began to sit them. I played tricks on her, stupid jokes, childish pranks, ill-suited to a thirty-one-year-old ex-teacher, encouraging her to sit a clutch of egg-sized potatoes, or a handful of like-sized pebbles from Cope's brook. She obliged each time, eager to sit and hatch even stones or pig potatoes.

Ernie Phillips, the only friend I had made during that winter, arriving one day with a bag of mill sweepings (seeds of nettles, docks and other unacceptable weeds found in corn) and two galvanised sheets, remarked on what he called the game of silly buggers I was playing with the hen. 'You should put her to good use instead of ramming odds and sods under her' he remarked, 'I'll bring you some real eggs, stuff worth hatching.' Stuff worth hatching – I knew what he meant. Ernie often did questionably legal delivery jobs for Nelson Jones, a tinker/scrap-dealer who had half-heartedly settled on the edge of the A5, and Nelson kept a strain of grey game fowl – not pretty enough to be show birds – the cock birds of which bore such hideous lacerations that any fool could have guessed why Nelson kept them.

Next day Ernie arrived with a dozen smallish white eggs which we slid under the sitting hen carefully removing her clutch of warm pig potatoes and grey pebbles. 'Call her Clara if I were you', remarked Ernie of the hen for no reason in particular, and left in his battered Morris van chugging his way back to Tamworth.

I've often wondered why Ernie decided to call the hen Clara. Perhaps he'd been forced into reading an infant school reader about a fat red hen called Clara, but the clutch my Silky was about to hatch was a far cry from the brood of fluffy yellow barnyard fowl discussed in infant story books. Jonesy prided himself on the ferocity of his birds and though I had never actually met him, he had infused Ernie with such tales of cut and thrust battles on tinker sites from here to Kirkcudbright, that it was easy to see why Ernie had offered to buy any chicks I might be able to hatch. Even in those days, the halcyon days of the never-had-it-so-good Macmillan years, when everyone but me was prosperous, Jones' grey cock birds were bought for as much as twenty pounds a piece by cockfighters. As it transpired however, my venture to provide combatants for grit and steel battles ended in disaster, which brings me back to my tale of the white-flighted sparrow-hawk.

Clara – and Ernie's name stuck – dutifully sat her clutch of eggs and hatched ten healthy normal chicks, undersized as are all game fowl chicks but healthy nevertheless, which is all the more amazing when one considered Jones had inbred the game fowl from the year dot.

Within weeks they had lost their appealing Easter-chick appearance and had developed a reptilian look as down gave way to hard feather, and Ernie was just about to work out how much Nelson would pay him for the brood when disaster struck.

One of the only skills I've ever picked up through my teaching experience is the ability to see a group of articles, animals etc and instantly assess the number which makes up the group. I've never understood calculus, and means, modes and medians, the latest craze in any modern day school maths syllabus, leaves me cold. However, I am easily capable of counting to ten and instantly able to detect when what should be ten is really nine. Thus when I whistled and clucked up Clara and her brood for this midday meal of mill sweepings I suddenly noticed one chick (or are they called poults at this age) was missing. Like the biblical good shepherd out to seek his one lost sheep, I meticulously searched the hedgerow, stamping down the batch of May nettles, but in vain. Next day however, the brood had dwindled to eight. All sorts of possibilities presented themselves.

I dismissed the idea of a fox being the culprit, as any self-respecting fox would have nabbed the hen and had done with it. Furthermore my half-blind terrier Sam, a demon with foxes and badgers was allowed to run with the chicks, and the presence of the dog in the run also ruled out the possibility of rats snatching up the chicks for Sam had one heck of a good reputation as a rat killer. The culprit was clearly an airborne predator, and while I've seen kestrels pick off day-old guinea fowl, a four-week-old game chick would be more than a match for a mouse-eating kestrel.

I saw my sparrow-hawk sitting on the branch of the oak tree that morning heavily camouflaged by leaves. She stared silently at the rapidly dwindling brood of poults. No creature can stare as hard or as meaningfully as a hawk, nor, I hasten to add, with such murderous intent. A hawk watches its prey, its movement, its mannerisms, assesses its chances of the prey escaping the first rush of wings and talons with such concentration that the hawk seems oblivious to the rest of the world as if hawk and prey were the only dwellers in the universe. A car may pass, a horse and dray go by, but a hawk will continue to watch its victim without so much as batting an eye. Such single-mindedness is to be admired (though it often brings about the death of the hawk) for I am unable to concentrate on any scene or subject for more than a few moments, but a hawk, particularly a sparrow-hawk is the best advert for Pelmanism yet devised. She continued to stare at the brood and her icy gaze left me in no doubt as to the future of the hatch of game fowl if I didn't shut them up during the daylight hours.

I hurriedly penned them up in my pallet- and orange-box-built shed, letting them out for only a matter of minutes per day while I fed them, but even this did not stop the attacks on the poults. For three days I kept the remaining chicks from harm, dropping the mill sweepings near my feet, discouraging any straying from the hen, but on the third day I saw a rush of wings out of the corner of my eye and the hawk flashed down from her perch snatching up a chick almost off the toe of my shoe. She lifted the poult skywards, dipped a little in her flight to get better purchase on her prey and flapped casually off to Cope's post where she began to dismantle the wretch alive. Screaming, cursing, throwing stones, sticks and anything to hand I raced across the road, but though she stared as though puzzled why I should take offence at her actions as I approached she simply lifted the half-plucked, still fluttering prey and flapped off to the tree near the railway embankment.

'Keep 'em up a few weeks, don't let 'em out till they're bigger,' Ernie suggested, 'and by the time they're ten weeks old they'll be big enough to fly up and attack the old bugger themselves', but to keep them up as Ernie put it was easier said than done. Two or three times she made putts at the frightened brood as I opened the door, coming low over my head, her talons almost brushing my ragged untidy hair. Her attacks mystified me and her lack of fear of humans made me think that she was quite simply a falconer's bird taken as an eyass hawk, trained and encouraged to lose her fear of man before she became lost on some hunting foray, and to this day I believe this to be so. Ernie however was not so convinced, and merely remarked rather scathingly that the hawk was simply able to spot a daft bugger like me as an easy touch. Still I kept her off the poults for another week, but one day a young cockerel, feathered enough to be almost attractive, hopped past me as I opened the shed door and she struck him before you could say 'knife'. She came so close to me that I aimed a kick at her causing her to miss her strike, but the hapless cockerel simply panicked and dashed further away from the protection of the shed, and she simply circled and picked him off with contemptuous ease.

She had to go of course, regardless of the rules of ecology, regardless of my vow to blend into the district, in spite of the legislation that demanded that no one should harm a hawk of any sort. Legislation, I reflected, was made in hawk-free London, a far cry from my shack in Huddlesford where I was desperately trying to preserve what game chicks remained. I walked to the scrap yard that morning cutting a Y shaped hazel twig on the way, and stripped a car tyre inner-tube to make a catapult; but I have never been a crack shot with a catapult or gun and after the first salvo of pebbles had sailed harmlessly past her, she ceased to perch on the oak tree and continued to make Blitzkrieg attacks from all angles reducing the brood to a mere half dozen and causing Ernie to throw up his hands in disgust at my lack of stockmanship and to cease bringing the mill sweepings.

Well, to cut a long story short, she saw off all my game chicks, an action that was more disconcerting to my geriatric mop of a foster mother than to me for I was not particularly enamoured with the prospect of rearing a batch of fighting fowl on the premises. Such a clutch attracts a variety of unsavoury characters, ranging from the slick type known as Spivs in post-war parlance, to tinkers, all eager to size up anything 'vaguely fightable' and literally anything 'moveable'. God knows I had little to steal but the amused glances of unwelcome visitors viewing my state of penury with disdain infuriated me. Thus with the extermination of the game chicks my premises became relatively quiet again, the peace disturbed only by the most incessant barking of my terrier and the unhappy cluck of Clara who laid two or three sterile white eggs and promptly went broody again.

By now I had decided to add yet another creature to my already overstocked menagerie, and thus I set out to trap, take and train my white-flighted sparrow-hawk.

It was of course, illegal to trap such a bird. In fact all birds of prey were protected at that time, but time and time again I had met falconers who had Scottish-bred peregrines – obtained via Home Office permit admittedly, but I have always detested the one law for the rich, one for the poor system which has undermined the very fibre of our society. If I had applied for a permit and mentioned my lack of success in the training of this the most difficult of hawks to master, if an established falconer had mentioned my impoverished state to the powers which grant licences, then I could have bet my bottom dollar that my request to take a sparrow-hawk would have been refused. Anyway at that time I had divorced myself from the rest of Britain to such a degree that my hundred-and-twenty-eight-yard strip of land almost constituted an independent state, and the hawk dwelled in the land over which I was king; so I cocked a snook at society and its class-orientated unfair laws and resolved to take my hawk sans permit. Besides that, by this time my relationship with her had become something of a blood feud, and to involve anyone else in my vendetta would have been something akin to sacrilege. I resolved that, without enlisting the aid of anyone else, I would trap my hawk and bend her to become an efficient hunting companion – and take her I did, though not I admit through my own artifices – but I jump the gun again I fear, and race ahead of my tale.

The first days of summer came and went, heralded by the curious green secondary foliage of the oak tree opposite my house, and I set out in deadly earnest to catch my hawk. A few weeks previously a young lad had brought me a fledgling thrush, for most of the district regarded me as a harmless St Francis type lunatic who was keen on taking in any crippled, damaged or unwanted creatures. I took it in, if only to watch with amazement as it opened its oversized yellow mouth to receive some insectivorous offering, and she (I've always assumed the bird was a hen) became quite tame and even welcomed me home with an incessant hopping around the house as I came through the front entrance of my shack. The rooms became daubed with white limey patches, and the house began to smell like a guano factory. Ernie returned that month finally coming to terms with the loss of his game chicks. 'You want to use that bloody thrush as bait for the trap' he muttered, finding that the one armchair in the house had become whitened with unmentionable and that same mess was now adhering to his clothes. For a moment I may have contemplated this use for my fledgling, but dismissed the idea immediately as I visualised a hawk's beak tearing into that feathered breast, decapitating that silly head, the mouth of which still gaped trustingly every time I entered the room. I shook my head at Ernie's suggestion and began constructing ridiculously Heath Robinson bow nets, elaborate unworkable box traps which failed to catch a single bird, but did a fair job at taking young squirrels. Summer wore on and though I checked the traps daily I found little to encourage my pursuing of this line of attack.

Clara went off her legs that September. She had sat clutch after clutch of potatoes, pebbles and other oddments, so much so that I believe it had damaged her leg structure. I checked an ancient copy of Wright's Book of Poultry, but there was little about ailing, geriatric Silky hens with a fixation about motherhood save that bringing an ailing hen into the warmth of a room sometimes worked miracles. I fetched her in, imprisoned in her Persil box container near to my smouldering wood fire and for a while she seemed to revive, but one morning I found her cold, lifeless and emaciated, her children's colouring book feathers caked with the filth she had evacuated at the moment of death. That same day my thrush chose to up sticks and leave home, if chose is the correct word for she trusted everyone and everything and would have been an easy victim for one of the cats which infested the district.

My spirits plummeted once again and I felt the same sense of despair I've always felt when one of my livestock dies. I am, I admit, a poor stock keeper for I become far too personally involved with my wards. A good stockman tries his hardest to ensure the health of his stock but shrugs off the death of his wards stoically. I was unable to accept these deaths and I began to busy myself, collecting branches for my wood pile, brushing the earth floor of my hovel and even attempting a cursory stab at cleaning my filthy, curtain-free windows. To the casual detached onlooker I must have resembled a deranged hamster or an autumnal squirrel with a fixation about the impending winter. Each day I worked solidly from dawn until evening but I am so disorganised by nature that at the end of a week I had little to show for my efforts.

Autumn came once again, wet and miserable, smelling of dead leaves, mildewed apples and decay. Each year is predictable in these parts, utterly predictable as though calendars were turned off by the same duplication year in year out, never changing and seldom varying. The cut of the corn will bring out the 'once-a-year hunters' armed with shotguns, and weeks later my ceiling will resound with the patter of the feet of rats driven out of the fields by the approaching winter. Leaf fall will bring the badgers scurrying around my waste bin, scuffing up my potato patch, frantically trying to gain enough fatty weight to last out the winter, and with the ripening of the thistle seeds near the Hurst Grove come the bird trappers from Walsall, Judas with call-birds in cages, and thick viscose bird-lime.

Each year they trap the grove, raping it of its finches and linnets, luring in the multicoloured wretches with their call-birds to feed amongst the thistles and to become gummed up with the strands of sticky esparto grass placed alongside the thistle stems. I watch them trap these birds each year, aware that what they are doing is not only illegal but probably damnably immoral, and though every fibre of my being should cry out about this pillage of my countryside, I am unmoved by the practice, treating it as part of the inevitable pattern of the seasons, as predictable and seasonal as leaf fall. A dozen species of bird fall prey to the Walsall trappers' artifices, finches of every kind, linnets and even sparrows; yet each year sees no apparent fall in the number of these birds I see nesting in the hedgerows that criss-cross these fields. Besides, these trappers too in their own slightly obnoxious way, are cocking the self-same snook at the law and the standards of society as I am, and as luck would have it they brought about the capture of my hawk.

I walked to the grove that morning endeavouring to see how much dead wood I could find on my way to the Hurst. It is a true saying that the lazy man works hardest, for I simply gathered wood by walking mile after mile around the lanes locally, whereas a concerted effort, a twenty-minute stint of hard chopping of the grove opposite my house would have yielded a week's burning. I turned into the grove opposite the Anchor Cottages, a ritzy residential set of lodges which have housed over these last sixteen years a variety of tenants, ranging from teeny-bop pop idols to characters which resembled extras from James Cagney films. A few fluttering finches, their feathers gummed, their wing flights stuck together, tried to make a half-hearted attempt at flapping their way out of my path. I watched them almost pityingly, wondering what fate awaited the poor devils. Many would not survive the first few days of incarceration, fretting in the same way as I would fret in the not so cosy confines of Winson Green Prison, a hell-hole some twenty miles south of my cottage. Others would see a variety of owners ranging from mule breeders out to produce somewhat dowdy, hardy but sterile little singers, ideally-suited for the lonely life in a draughty kitchen. Others would become unwilling pets, singing their heads off in boredom in some Black Country council house, a far cry from the alders of Whittington Hurst. I watched the wretches scuttle like crabs failing to get airborne and finally giving up the ghost as I approached gathering my wood, and then quite suddenly I saw her, my hawk, my long-term adversary, gummed up with slime, still able to flutter from branch to branch but grounded nevertheless. I raced after her watching her unfurl her white-flighted wings in a vain attempt to get lift off, but her efforts degenerated to an ungainly hop, twixt branches. I'd seen many large birds stuck up with lime, but never incapacitated enough to render them grounded. What amazing new hell-brew had these bird trappers come up with to 'down' a fully grown sparrow-hawk, I wondered at the time, but I had little time to ponder on the subtle alchemy of the mix for I had taken off my thread-bare donkey coat and was endeavouring to throw it over her to render her 'hors de combat' so to speak.

The quote of leviathan with a hook flashed to mind; a huge or mighty adversary laid low by some simple artifact. For months I had tried my damnedest to catch her, dreamed up Machiavellian plans to bring her to hand, drawn up plans of machines and traps which would have set a Leonardo wondering, and now she had been laid low by some low-grade mix of rat lime which some amateur bird trapper had set out on thistles to take small passerines. I made one final lunge at her with my donkey coat and felt her struggling body beneath the cloth. Never have I raced home more quickly. It is curious but a few weeks ago I went once more to the grove and found the pile of rotting wood I had dropped some sixteen years ago. Nothing seems to change around here except that each year the housing estates come one step nearer and I become more wrinkled, grey-haired and crochety.

I was of course totally unprepared to train my catch. To tame – a curious word when applied to hawks – a haggard, a wild caught bird with an almost paranoid fear of man requires not only considerable patience, but a sight more equipment. To start with, one needs jesses, strips of leather cut to fit the hawk's legs. Hoods I could dispense with for I have never become deft enough to be able to perform the conjurer's trick called hooding a hawk – though I am told by those who should know that for some reason it is easier to hood a haggard than a nestling eyass; but above all I lacked the darkened room so often recommended by books concerning falconry. A room where light which would trigger off a memory of the hawk's freedom could not disturb the bird and send it into a paroxysm of frenzy to escape from her captors. Falconers or austringers would start by sitting next to the bird, sitting stock still in the darkness of the room, and allowing in more and more light as the bird became less afraid and more accustomed to her trainer. However, I am rarely prepared for emergencies and I confess I had given up hope of trapping my hawk anyway.

Other folk seem to lead neat, orderly lives, everything in its place and a place for everything. My own world is invariably chaotic. The arrival of a litter of puppies usually finds me scurrying around the dog kennels to make place for the new arrivals. Likewise these days the first day of term finds me totally unprepared for my timetable commitments for, as I've said, I've never been a good teacher, and now on reflection perhaps I was never destined to be even a moderate falconer.

I hurried home and turned her loose in the bedroom while I raced around finding an old enamelled advertisement board which advertised extinct and seemingly antiquated and outmoded products, to nail over the window. The end result was a ghastly mess which left me sweating, cursing and bleeding slightly. Still, it kept out just some of the light and turned the room into a perpetually twilight world, a shadowy world which I now realise must have been more terrifying to a hawk than bright sunlight, but in my exhilaration to construct a mews, for this is what my Heath Robinson room was called in hawking parlance, I had not realised this. Jesses I made from the pair of shoe-laces my cousin Janet bought me when she sort of called in to see me in my wretchedness, and finding that I had nothing of any value to my name decided to ameliorate my squalor by donating a pair of bootlaces. I still went laceless and cut down Janet's present to make jesses for my captive. A coal sack left by Ernie when he delivered his mill sweepings made a screen perch, and the swivel I cut out of one of Sam's old and rotten leads.

A length of binder twine left in a hedgerow by some hay-feeding farmer became the leash and also a creance, and with my hawk equipped thus, looking as shabby and down-at-heel as myself, I set to train her, sitting with her in the darkness of the mews, occasionally talking to her as she shuffled nervously on her perch, but sitting for the most part in silence contemplating my lot in life.

I own a car now, a ramshackle Fiat 126, the gear box of which is falling away from the rest of the engine, but in those days I went everywhere on foot. These days I worry about how I will get the money to pay for the vehicle's frequent repairs, but in those days some sixteen years ago I was incredibly rich for I needed nothing. Karl Marx I believe said something about the ownership of all property being theft, but really Marx had it all wrong. When a person develops middle-class values there is always so much more that he needs, or rather wants, for the difference twixt needs and wants has become a little obscure these days. At that time I needed nothing – a greater quantity of binder twine perhaps, but little more. I've always been different and I've paid the price of being different, but I've steadfastly refused to accept the values of other people. As a schoolboy I was regarded as a little strange, in college as quite simply 'bats' and in the teaching profession, so peculiar that every head I'd worked for seemed almost desperate to see me gone. Quasi-psychiatrists, only a shade more bizarre than the real McCoy, state that one of the first signs of mental instability is when someone considers that he alone is marching in time and the rest of the world are out of step. If this is correct I admit I'm stark staring mad, for I consider that the rest of the world is out of time, for I believe my values are correct and the fast-buck theology which has permeated society is not only wrong, but the most destructive force the human race has yet dreamed up. Modern man, stress-damaged, worried about mortgages and what the neighbours will say is only half alive, and in those days I was at peace with myself – prone to bouts of depression maybe, but relatively on an even keel. One day I met a villager who called me 'bats' to my face, then only a month later put his head in the gas oven because he couldn't keep up the mortgage payments. There is a Czech fairy tale, one with a sting in its tail, about a village, the life of which centred around a well. One day someone poisoned the well and sent the people completely mad – all except the head man who hadn't touched the water. He alone remained sane, but the rest of the villagers lamented the fact that the head man, because he didn't think as they did, was crazy. One day he drank the waters and he too became mad – and the people rejoiced because their leader had regained his sanity. Now, when I reflect on the penury of those days, and my present relative prosperity as a Scale III teacher, I realise the meaning of that curious fairy tale. My sense of values at that time was correct, and I lost those values and drank the water of the fairy-tale well when I was forced to return to teaching. Self-sufficiency enthusiasts referred to as self-sufficiency 'freaks' by the unkind unenlightened world, people who get away from it all living on a shoe-string but doing their own thing, are the only sane people in this crazy world for life is too short to be ruled by the values of other folk. Sitting there alone in the darkness listening to that damned bird shuffling on its perch preparing itself for a bate I came to know myself better than at any other time in my life, but, philosophising is one thing and training a hawk is another; so I resume my tale.

Few recently-trapped hawks eat during the first few days of captivity. Most are hell-bent on escaping, all are so terrified of man that to take food, even freshly-killed birds, is anathema, and it is only after four or five days that hunger begins to bite and the hawk shows an interest in the food offered it. However, to train any hawk it is necessary to keep the bird in a state of hunger which would delight a potential anorexic. No hawk is biddable until it has lost roughly a tenth of its natural body weight. Thus a large female sparrow-hawk which weighs maybe ten and a half ounces when captured needs to be reduced to roughly nine ounces before it becomes even reasonably biddable. Here is the rub however – drop the weight too quickly or worse still drop the weight too much, and in next to no time you have a dead hawk on your hands. Few falconers will openly admit to having a hawk die from what is frankly simply malnutrition, but many must have simply misjudged the weight of hawks and paid the inevitable price for their mistake. To keep a sparrow-hawk in condition with daily weighing is a bit of a task. To train one simply by gauging its weight is a nightmare. I had no scales at that time, still don't for that matter, so I had to assess the right weight for my female simply by watching her body condition and noting her eagerness to feed each time I appeared.

Funnily enough she trained reasonably quickly and though she refused to come straight to the fist she would fly quite readily to the lure and allow me to pick her up. I'd like to be able to say that we developed an amicable relationship, the hawk, my terrier and myself, and that we jelled into a supreme hunting trio, but it would be a lie. She was a nervous bird; a lifetime in the wilds where she could observe man's predatory, destructive ways had done little to instil confidence in her, and although she became obedient and reasonably well-trained I always had the feeling that she disliked me – hated and loathed me would be more accurate, and I thought if she could, she would have gladly killed me leaving my body a macerated mess before she took her leave of me. Most days I would watch her in her mews and talk to her using the same nonsensical drivel falconers have spoken to hawks since man first caught a bird of prey to train. While I had only to move to find her staring intently at me, in her quieter moments she would gaze out of the window at the fields behind my house, fields she had hunted without the encumbrance of jesses, and as I watched her I realised that her incarceration in my shabby bedroom was not only illegal but damnably wrong of me. Thus it was that I decided to train her, fly her at birds a few times and then release her, seeing her pass my house occasionally, greeting her as cordially as one treats a once-loved mistress, regarding the whole enterprise as simply a test of my skill as a trainer of animals, but as Burns says, the best laid plans of mice and men. I'd love to be able to say that I trained and tamed my harridan and we became inseparable companions growing old together, her flying blackbirds and partridges galore in true expert falconry-book manner, but it would be a lie. The truth is that I kept her nearly twelve weeks and flew her at one blackbird with success. I say success with reservation for though she managed to catch and kill her prey I felt mildly foolish, mean and more than a little sadistic about the enterprise, for as soon as I released the hawk and she flew to a tree to still-hunt, the blackbird refused to leave the hedgerow and became so terrified that I had to dislodge the poor devil with my hands to make him fly. I watched her crash down on him, heard his shrill plaintive twitter as she dispatched him and felt very guilty about the whole business. Far from being in tune with my environment, I was out of kilter with it. If she had flown and killed a partridge I could have eaten it and allowed her to dine on any surplus – the head, neck etc. As it was I had spent an hour hunting a tiny blackbird, inedible and useless to me though my hawk had shredded the creature hungrily. Something was horribly wrong and having concluded that I had proved I could train such a hawk I decided to release her the very next day. However, when the time came to turn her loose I gazed at her plumage, her wild eyes, her sharp eager manner, admired the almost reptilian beauty of the creature and like Bedivere with the sword of the dying Arthur, I just couldn't let her go.

Two days later I walked into Lichfield to catch a bus for Walsall Wood, the purpose of my trip being to get Ernie to deliver a load of old galvanised iron sheets which I would use to fence in my duck run. I sat in Lichfield bus station cafe, ate a bun and drank tea, my first civilised meal since I purchased Clara. Opposite me was a decidedly hippy-like girl, the type that twenty years ago was called a beatnik. She too was a drop-out, a pitiful inadequate with no ambitions and no hope for the future. We talked about meaningless things, made trite conversation about Jean Paul Sartre, about Chagal and a host of other subjects about which I knew precious little and she knew even less and the outcome of the situation was that when I returned from Walsall Wood I spent the night at my beatnik's flat.

I couldn't recall her name even if I tried and I admit I've never tried and all I can remember about the relationship was that her room looked like a bomb-site or perhaps a training area for the SAS, a nasty mess of esoteric books and dirty clothes liberally stained with coffee and tea residues and a smell that resembled the laundry basket of a woman with a large number of unwashed children. Her conversation became inane and the only noteworthy comment of the evening was that if she had had a child she didn't want she'd call the brat Horace regardless of its sex.

I mulled over the stupidity of the statement as I walked home next morning remembering it was Groucho Marx who said that he wouldn't consider joining any club which would accept him as a member. Likewise I couldn't respect any woman who would consider me as a bed-mate in my state of wretchedness. Suddenly I began to feel very unclean about the whole nasty, sordid little business and quickened my pace to drive all thoughts of this stupid woman from my head. I have known many stupid women and many sleazy women I confess, but this woman had an unwholesome brand of sleaziness blended with a singularly nasty unhealthy type of stupidity. I felt a sudden revulsion for her, and her parting words inviting me back again that night made me feel contemptuous of myself. Throughout my spell of penury, my stint of transcendentalism, I had lived I confess, in squalor, but in spite of scabies and headlice I had managed to keep my self-respect. Now I felt spiritually unclean. I scurried along the frosty road to my house, my donkey coat collar tucked up until I resembled a very seedy, rustic, down-at-heel version of a Dasheil Hammitt hero out to investigate a turnip theft.

I quickened my pace as I crossed the canal bridge and a strange premonition hit me like an icy shower. It was twelve noon and five hours past my hawk's feeding time. Five hours – not a long time for a goshawk and a twinkling of an eye for a fat contented eagle, but for a sparrow-hawk, for a bird scarcely nine ounces in weight, a hawk kept fine with her appetite honed to a razor sharpness, it was an aeon of time. I had fed her little the day previous quite simply because I had found only a road casualty dead hedge-sparrow during my walks around the lanes. It would not have been enough to keep even a small musket fit and well. Furthermore, the night had been chilly, the sort of damp, spiteful chilliness one associates with early spring, a time of the year when winter seems reluctant to release its icy grip on the land. Such a freezing night coupled with my hawk's low condition could have done her considerable harm.

I pushed open the door (I didn't lock up my house at that time for I had nothing to steal) and practically ran to the bedroom, waiting by the door a while in the hopes of hearing that shuffling motion she used when she was well and truly ready for her meal. The room was silent except for a gentle tapping sound and I found her hanging, head down, by her leash, her brilliant red eyes now glassy and fish-like, her body twisting and turning slightly with every draught like the pendulums of those very 'with it' rotary clocks. I felt very bad about the whole messy business, the wasted night, the death of the bird through malnutrition, but more particularly because I didn't really want to keep the bird and all I needed to do was to give her a full gorge of food, turn her loose and in minutes she would have been as wild as though she had never known captivity.

I buried her in the hedgerow over which she must have hunted a hundred times or more. Once again I took stock of my situation, and quite suddenly for the first time in my life, I felt very old.

LUPINE EYE

—6—

Reflections In A Lupine Eye

ZOOS DEPRESS ME, any form of captivity, whether it be the awful imprisonment imposed by some forms of domestication or the incarceration of man or beast disturbs me. Indeed, the only reason I have stayed clear of any serious encounter with the law is, not because I am a basically honest person (believe me I am not) but simply because of my near-claustrophobic dread of being enclosed. Mine is a fearsome claustrophobia, for I feel suffocated and restricted even when I am forced to travel through a city. Thus zoos, with their stock of listless, bored and captive creatures, denied their natural freedom, cause my manic-depressive pendulum to hit an all-time zero.

Curiously, the sight of lions, tigers, or panthers sitting out their lives in tiny enclosures, awaiting even a slight variation in their next meal to break the awful monotony, does not particularly worry me, but the vision of foxes restlessly moving to and fro in wired in enclosures, ceaselessly pacing back and forth to lend some spice to their bland existence has a decidedly depressing effect on me. Zoo lovers state, in defence of these menageries, that such beasts are spared the rigours the wild offers, the anguish and terror of the chase, the agony of death at the jaws of some predator, the gnawing pangs of hunger when a hunt has been unsuccessful; but these are poor rewards for the freedom they have lost. Esau traded his birthright for a mess of pottage, so the story goes, but how much more have these creatures bartered for their snug, air-conditioned, antiseptic prisons.

Foxes, wolves and jackals seem most ill-at-ease in these menageries, and invariably spend their miserable, wretched lives fretting for an unobtainable freedom. Alas, unobtainable seems to be the operative word, with every year seeing a rash of new suburbs submerging and crushing the wild which once harboured these beasts. But then I am a canophile, a dog lover, I suppose, so perhaps I naturally identify with these wild canids.

Or do I? As I gaze almost hypnotised into the sleepy, golden eye of the European wolf, the nervous, quicksilver pupils of foxes or at the furtive, oriental glances of jackals, somehow I am aware that I am not looking at the ancestors of the dog which sits at my feet as I write. Of one thing I am certain, these wild creatures are not the same beasts which shared some dark cave with my ancestors, sitting out the blackness of the pre-quarternary nights. In my heart of hearts I know this to be true, for in spite of my near-fascination, no, near-obsession would be more correct, with wolves and all things lupine, I know that these were not the beasts men tamed to help man become the most feared predator that has walked the face of the earth. The early dogs which shared those caves with a more simple type of man were not ill-tamed wolves, for mankind is not sympatico with the ways of wolves. Even in the mists of early legend the wolf is portrayed as a beast to fear, hostile to man, alien to the ways of humans. He is the story-book creature, the beast of the twilight, the creature that haunts the darkness, awful in his savaging, terrifying in his cunning, and if historic man equipped with fire and spears to drive away these beasts regarded the wolf with such awe, how much more would prehistoric man, pre-Promethean man, have feared him. There was no reason to try and tame this beast, for he was always the creature which dwelled in the shadowy mists of legend rather than by the camp-fires of primitive man.

Perhaps, if man can unravel the mystery of the domestication of the dog, he will come near to the understanding of his own evolution, for the domestication of dogs and the evolution of man are intertwined so closely, that to understand one, one must know much of the other. In the quiet times – and as I grow older these quiet times grow more and more important to me – when I gaze into the flickering lights of a fire, and feel the shapes mesmerise me, I reach down and touch the ears of one of my dogs and feel a strange psychometry, a curious link with the past, induced by the flickering and changing shapes within the flames. It is perhaps fanciful to imagine that I am allowed these glimpses into man's pre-history, but perhaps the quiet times, the proximity of the dog at my feet and the hypnotic effect of the blazing branches of the fire, unlocks some archetypal imagery and allows me glimpses of a time so distant, so ancient, so antique as to make the building of the pyramids seem recent.

In the ever-changing shapes within the fire I see man, primitive man, more ape-like than human, leaving the trees to walk with tottering two-legged strides on the savannah, the hostile grassland below the trees. But it was not the fear of the great apes who ruled the trees that drove man from those branches, for the savannah was a million times more hostile and dangerous than the trees, which this creature who was destined to be man, had left behind. Something deep within those ape-like men, borne in the flames of my fire, compelled them to leave the branches and walk upon the plains below the trees. Forget the quasi-human, timid ape-like man seen in sci-fi films. My tree-dweller, he who would be lord of all the earth, was a furious beast, aggressive towards other creatures (and perhaps even his own kind) long before he left the branches, and he was armed and mentally equipped to become the arch-predator long before he left the trees. Man came down walking on two legs, not four, not because he could move more easily with bipedal strides – he couldn't – but because by dint of walking on his hind legs he could wield weapons in his fore-paws. Weapons – well, sticks, stones, jawbones of gazelles perhaps, but weapons nevertheless and the precursors of the ICBMs of today. In the firelight I watch him stalking the herds in some African Eden, pulling down the weak, the aged, the helpless, cleansing the species of any unsuitable and superfluous stock, and somewhere out on the savannah he was watched, feared and held in awe by the ancestors of the lurcher which lies at my feet as I sit and watch the fire tell its tale.

There would have been hard times for this Dawn Man, times when his very species tottered on the brink of extinction, for man was as yet the embryonic hunter, the incomplete hunter, content during times of scarcity to scavenge alongside the vulture and the hyena, content to forage for nuts and roots with the herds of primitive swine which rooted in the earth of that fast-drying savannah. Man must have balanced along the slender arrête of extinction for an aeon of time while he learned the skills to become a competent and efficient hunter. Perhaps a dozen quasi-human types left the trees during that time, but one species alone, or at the most two, were destined to survive. The rest – well they went the way of the Mylodon and the Tomarctus, creatures which nearly made it. Why the creature which scientists in their wisdom are wont to call *Homo Sapiens* survived is open to conjecture. My own theory is that he was the only one of those ape-like beasts who formed a relationship with dog-like creatures, who watched his amateurish attempts at hunting during those inhospitable times.

These primitive dogs too scavenged when times were hard, but they were not omnivorous enough to be called jackals, not predatory enough to be called wolves, and if man walked the tight-rope of extinction during those times so did the primitive ancestors of our dogs.

How man and dog teamed up will always be debated, but team up they did. Perhaps at first to the mutual benefit of both, though later, man true to character, was certain to welch on the deal. Men have better eyesight than dogs, better even than the best of sight hounds, but the dog contributed speed, nose and a hunting instinct maybe two or three million years more developed than that of man's. My bet is that dogs teamed up with men simply because man is the furious predator, a creature who stands alone amongst beasts because he kills for sport as much as to satiate his hunger, and his hauls usually far exceed his needs. The primitive ancestors of our dogs were faced with a decision to join up with man and form what scientists call a symbiotic relationship, a partnership helpful to both, or to go it alone and reject the company of the stick wielding, two-legged apes. Those dogs which teamed up survived, the others – well, they went on balancing along the tight-rope of extinction for maybe a hundred thousand years or so and then they too became extinct. So the strange bond between dog and man, the most unlikely of partnerships, became welded together and slowly the two independent hunters united to form the most formidable of combinations, having the speed and nose of the dog and the ruthless cunning of the creature about to emerge as true man. The time to go forth and inherit the earth was at hand.

But the time of leaving that African Utopia was also at hand. The once luxurious plains, lush with vegetation, thick with herds of edible game, were drying up. The rains no longer came at their appointed times, and the deserts began to inch their way into the once fertile land. The time to leave this African Garden of Eden was at hand and man and his fellow predators followed the migrating herds to colder climes, and in these colder climes man and his canine companions met and came into competition with wolves. Perhaps some lupine blood did enter into the canine stock at that time, but it would have been a chance introduction, not one that was fostered and encouraged by man. An accidental mating twixt a dog-hungry in-season bitch and an outcast elderly wolf might have produced a litter or so of whelps, but wolves regard stray dogs as meat rather than mates. Look at the studded collar sported by Staffordshire bull terriers or at the cartoon Tom and Jerry bulldogs. These collars are a relic of a time when shepherd and guard dogs wore spiked collars as a protection against marauding wolves. In fact trappers in Canada and Siberia seem reluctant to have a dog accompany them on their expeditions as the presence of a dog lures in wolves to the camp-site, wolves which incidentally are interested in the dog as a source of food. There's a tale about a girl called Katie Adams who lived in Alberta in the 1880s and owned a pet collie. One day she found herself surrounded by a family of timber wolves, which ignored the ten-year-old child, but attacked and ate her collie.

Believe me there is little proof that such matings were common and no proof that man actively encouraged this hybridising. Wolf blood had nothing to contribute to the hunting ability of those early dogs. Wolves are aloof, remote beasts, intractable, unwilling and perhaps unable to bend to man's will, and while certain cynologists, Lorenz in particular, seem to delight in this aloof lupine disposition, such intractability would have ensured that man would have been unsuccessful in his hunting. Early dogs needed to be malleable and ductile, obedient beasts, to assist man in his hunting and later in his herding activities, and there would have been no room for any dog which did not bend to man's will and become utterly biddable and controllable during a hunt. Wolves are certainly not biddable, and contrary to the views of Degenbø, who believes that dogs are simply wolves which have undergone changes during domestication, early man, always on the very brink of famine, would have had little time to practice eugenics and breed a more versatile and biddable wolf to become his hunting companion.

So my views are not shared by most cynologists, but then few of my opinions are shared by others. A cynologist – I'd best explain that word, it means a serious student of dogs and dog behaviour – called ironically Wolfgramin, started experimenting with wolves in 1894. Wolfgramin argued that if wolves were taken out of the wild, kept in unnatural conditions from puppyhood (or cubhood), various changes took place and these even affected the wolf's skeleton making its head shorter and making it smaller in size than its wild counterpart. Lorenz, in his superb book *Man Meets Dogs*, states that he believes two types of dog exist, the easily trained type of dog, the best example of which is the Alsatian or German Shepherd Dog which Lorenz stated was descended from the Golden Jackal, and the more aloof untrainable dog, the sort which misinformed people proudly state has a character of its own (Lorenz states the best example of this is the Chow Chow) which Lorenz calls a lupine dog as he believes it was descended from the wolf, *canis lupus*. At the risk of offending these experts in dog behaviour may I state that I believe that the wolf contributed nothing to the breeding of the modern domesticated dog. Man did not tame the remote and aloof northern wolf to become the biddable dog we know today. That dog he brought out of Africa, a tractable, docile dog, sycophantic, easy-going and as easily trainable then as now, ready-made and hand-tailored for the hunt.

Yet, though the wolf did not creep near the camp-fires of paleolithic man, he seeped insidiously into his legends and his folklore. The fox of fairy tales is the brash, sly, gauche villain, easily tricked by those with wits enough to take him, yet the wolf is always depicted as another type of foe. He is the velvet-voiced assassin, the riddler who allows man to gamble for the ultimate stake. He is the rapacious trap set for the unwary, the destroyer of those foolish enough to venture abroad after the setting sun has called its curfew. He is the 'dweller in the darkness', as much a part of the night as the starlight. Legend depicts him as an apocalyptic horseman, the devourer of those left alone in the house at night, a creature with more than mere animal intelligence. Truly, man migrating north from those fast-drying African plains, must have feared this great grey master of the northern tundra. At first, wolves would have feared man, been alarmed by the alien barking of the camp curs, been terrified by the firelight; but as time went on they would have become aware that man was the weakest of prey, the most easily slain of all the beasts of the chase. Alarmed, alone, away from the camp-fires and the watchful camp cur dogs, man became prey and easy prey at that, and while it was possible to keep the wolf away from the camp-fires, he would find his way into the folklore of man and become instilled in the very fibres of primaeval fear, seeping like a pale miasma into the nightmares of men, becoming some of the pieces that constituted the jigsaw puzzle of a frightful archetypal dream.

These were my opinions of wolves before I began to embark on a serious study of them. Some ten years ago I became besotted with the idea of breeding my own strain of dog, having a breed called after me, so to speak. Lorenz believes that the creation of new breeds is an open field for anyone with time or money to experiment (I should add that I had merely time), and suggests that a dazzling beautiful and useful breed might be created by mating collies with chow chows. However at that time I resolved that the breed I would create would be a more bizarre type of creature. As a child I absorbed the stories of Henry Treece and Rosemary Sutcliffe like a sponge, tales of Celtic heroes unbridled by Christianity, living hunting, shooting, fighting existences in the thickly forested land of pre-Roman Britain. Like as not each super-hero was accompanied by a dog, a huge hairy beast as big as a young calf, fierce to my heroes' enemies, a wondrous hunter capable of pulling down just about any prey and a guard dog to put Cerberus to shame. Without exception these super-dogs, suitable partners for men like Finn and Cuhullain, were what was called 'wild bred' – the result of staking an in-season wolf-hound bitch in the forests and allowing her to couple with wolves. I became besotted with the idea of breeding such a beast and my own lurcher paled into a pathetic shadow of a dog alongside such story-book hounds.

Well, the years passed, but like Peter Pan I refused to grow up, and when at last I became relatively settled in my tumbledown cottage I resolved to set to and breed such a creature. On reflection it was an illogical idea, and how to dispose of surplus puppies would certainly prove a problem. There would be little market for a litter of dog/wolf hybrids of that I was sure, and the eccentrics who fancied such a pup/cub call them what you will, would be few and far between.

Track record-wise there seemed little evidence to suggest that such hybrids existed or could be bred. At that time Lorenz was beginning to recant his theory that the chow chows were bred down from wolf stock and I was having serious doubts about the findings of Wolfgramin. Both Aristotle and Oppian (a mate of Julius Caesar so the tale goes) believed that wolves mated quite freely with dogs. In fact Aristotle goes one stage further and states that five different kinds of wolf coupled quite readily with dogs. Sadly Aristotle goes just a stage too far and mentions that in India certain strains of hound were the result of tying in-season bitches in the jungle and allowing them to mate with tigers. At that point Aristotle lost credibility as far as I was concerned, and though a tiger/dog hybrid would make a wonderful burglar deterrent for my all too often pillaged house, I couldn't really believe such hybrids could be produced, and after reading such garbage I had doubts about the existence of wolf/dog hybrids as well. In Aristotle's curious little world beasts of all kinds were simply tumbling into bed with each other regardless of differences in chromosome numbers and mating habits.

Hubbard's excellent little *Observer's Book of Dogs*, a tiny volume that was my first book and set me on the glorious down-hill path (so my Mother says) makes mention of a strain of sled-dog, bred from mating sled-dog bitches to wolves. These wolf-dogs were supposed to be the ultimate sled-dogs, capable of whipping even an unwilling team of huskies into shape, in half the time it took Buck of *Call of The Wild* fame. However when Riddle questioned old-time Malemute (a type of husky) breeders, Indians and Eskimos about these dogs no one admitted to having deliberately mated wolves with dogs to breed sled-dogs. The chances are that now and again a particularly lupine (wolf-like) puppy would appear in a sled-dog litter, and quick as a flash its owner would invent a spurious pedigree for the beast in the same manner as lurcher breeders are wont to do, when trying to sell a dog.

On the subject of Malemutes, which to my untutored eye look as near to wolves in appearance as dammit is to swearing, Mrs Robert Russell, wife of the President of the Alaskan Malemute Club of America, told Riddle who collected an interesting heap of folklore on dogs and wolves that she once reared a captive-bred wolf cub with a litter of Malemutes and Abasengi. (Apparently there is a considerable market for wolf cub 'pets' in America – here the sale of these would be prohibited or at least regulated in Britain by the Dangerous Animals Act of 1973.)

As a cub, 'Daffney' as the Russells called the wolf cub was a charming if nervous pet, more given to hiding than attacking when strangers appeared. All the dogs dominated her, taking her food, treating her as the bottom rung of the pecking order scale. As time went by however, the schism between dogs and wolf widened and the Malemutes came to fear her, avoiding her even when she was in heat. Mrs Russell also mentioned a near-season Malemute bitch's attempt to flirt with a captive wolf male. She made the mistake of attempting an appeasement gesture by placing her foot through the chain-link fencing to touch him and he promptly proceeded to gnaw off her leg. This however sometimes happens when a terrier gets its foot through the wire of a neighbouring terrier's cage.

However, not every cynologist (that word again) is of the opinion that dogs will not mate and conceive with wolves. Take for instance the naturalist C. H. D. Clarke. Clarke made a study of wolves and cases of wolf attacks on humans in Europe and Central Asia, where stories of wolves killing men abound, and came to a rather startling and somewhat controversial conclusion. All attacks made on humans by wolves could be attributed to either rabid wolves or to wolf/dog hybrids. Clarke kicks off with the tale of the Beasts of Gevaudan, a pair of wolves which created havoc in the Cevênnes Mountains of France between the years 1764 and 1767 and saw off at least sixty-four people and some say over a hundred. Hunters arrived from all over Europe to catch the pair and slew over two thousand innocent (I wonder whether innocent is the correct word when applied to this subject) wolves but still the attacks continued. Eventually a crotchety old man called Antoine de Bauterne, a man nearer seventy than sixty, set out and slew both beasts. The male weighed 130 lbs and stood 32 inches at the shoulder (a record for any European or Asiatic wolf) and had such unusual markings that Clarke concludes the beast was a dog/wolf hybrid made more dangerous because the 'dog' blood made the beast unafraid of man. Funnily enough, Riddle mentions that when Fox and Lockwood were successful in mating Malemutes with wolves, the hybrids usually weighed in at up to 20 lbs more than either parent.

Another curious looking 'wolf' which Clarke believed to be a hybrid is the most legendary beast 'Courtaud', which besieged Paris in the year 1430, a time when France was having a rather bad time from invading English ruffians who behaved a little like English football supporters with swords. At that time Paris was situated on an island in the river Seine and cattle had to be driven along miles of roads to get to the city. On one bank of the Seine were hundreds of caves where wolves bred in number (this area boasts an art gallery called the Louvre but originally the area was called the 'Louvrier' or the place where wolves breed – you're a font of useless information Plummer). It is believed that Courtaud, a hybrid twixt a shepherd dog male and a female wolf so story has it, was whelped on some neighbouring farm. Courtaud had a bobtail like many of the local sheepdogs but was of a great size, and so unafraid of men that he led packs of wolves in attacks on drovers trying to enter the city. Paris was held in a state of seige for several months until, in despair, the mayor of Paris ordained that animals should be gutted, bled and a trail of cadavers and entrails made to lure Courtaud and his fellow wolves into the city. Once into the city the wolves found their exits blocked and an army of citizens and soldiers set to and beat Courtaud and his brethren to death.

Meanwhile back at the ranch, my own experiments on hybridising dogs and wolves were about to take place. I'd read an article concerning wolves written by a fascinating eccentric called Dr John Naylor, one of the few scientists who can actually put an interesting story together without getting lost in a maze of unbelievably long $64,000 words. Naylor's article made out that the wolf, far from being the devourer of small pigs and grandma-fixated unpleasant little girls in red cloaks, was a timid creature which was having a hell of a time from being persecuted by human beings. What interested me most however was that Naylor had actually bred wolves in a backyard type garden on a young executive type estate, telling his neighbours that the beasts patrolling in the wire compounds were really alsatians so as not to alarm the '2.4 children typical executive families'. Frankly there would have been hell to pay if the locals had realised what Naylor was breeding in that enclosure – if one keeps ferrets in such an area there is usually a hue and cry about it at the Tenants' Association meetings. Naylor had however succeeded in rearing three litters of cubs from his wards, and after much fuss and bother with the editor of the periodical that published Naylor's article, I was given Naylor's address after I'd promised not to 'shop' the wolf keeper to the local council. I wrote to Naylor forthwith telling him I'd like a crack at mating a mongrel collie/alsatian to his male Siberian grey wolf and received a reply from him inviting me over to see his menagerie.

Naylor's wolf pen – I was almost about to write wolf pit, as Anglo Saxons with an aversion to stray Vikings kept such pits well stocked with hungry wolves lest a lost Norseman or so should drop in – was not surprisingly quite small; what was surprising was that the occupants of his private zoo were in good condition and immaculately kept. Contrary to popular belief, big cats such as lions, tigers, leopards etc don't seem to suffer much in small enclosures, for cats are not particularly energetic creatures, sleeping sometimes twenty hours a day, usually galvanising into action only when they need to bring about a kill. Wolves, jackals and particularly foxes need huge enclosures, for they are restless beasts pacing to and fro incessantly like a school teacher awaiting a Scale IV interview. How Naylor kept these wolves in an enclosure scarcely bigger than my Dobermann run is a puzzle. How he managed to get them to breed in such a tiny compound and successfully rear the cubs is more a mystery.

The two bitch wolves were hardly impressive, both looking rather like the dogs one sees around the villages in Northern India with perhaps just a dash of alsatian thrown in for good measure. Both looked in superb coat, and frankly good coat is the best indication as to the true condition of wild canids, but had the gaunt, faraway look of the Red Riding Hood wolf of children's story books. The male was a different matter. Naylor had had the good fortune to obtain a fine specimen of Siberian grey wolf, the sort that is usually seen knocking eight bells out of a troika filled with anxious hunters in Eastern European Bloc films. He scaled in at about 95 lbs which is big for a European or Asiatic wolf. Wolves look deceptively heavy and although one Canadian park ranger killed a giant weighing in at 172 lbs, that is one whole lot of wolf, and European wolves rarely if ever top 90 lbs in fit but scrawny condition. Naylor's wolf stood a good six inches taller than my cross-bred collie bitch that I had decided to use as a victim-cum-guinea-pig for the experiment, and bearing in mind I had read the Russells' account of wolves eating the leg from a live malemute (90–100 lbs of hard canine flesh) my collie/alsatian could have been in for a whole load of trouble if Naylor's wolf had been ill-disposed toward her. Explaining the death of the bitch would also present a bit of problem as I'd borrowed her from an old lady in the village, blatantly lying my head off by saying that I really fancied her (the dog not the old lady) and I'd love a puppy from her and a very quiet alsatian yet another friend owned. Anyway I was on my uppers financially at the time and I didn't particularly want the problem of trying to sell a litter of collie/alsatian/wolf hybrids which would attract a crowd of weirdos found only in Woody Allen films, so I resolved to get the bitch mated, take a puppy/cub for my troubles, allow the old lady to sell the remaining litter to unsuspecting good homes, keep a check on where they went and plot a graph of the mayhem such hybrids would create. The prospect of telling the old lady my friend's quiet alsatian had killed her pet and eaten its leg off did cause me some concern I admit, but I've always decided to cross bridges when I come to them.

Naylor seemed a little puzzled at my proposed experiment and asked what I hoped to gain by introducing wolf genes into a strain of domesticated dog, and quite honestly I was, I admit, stuck for a reply. Fox and Zimen, two American zoologists, had supposedly pulled off this cross in the 1970s, and though many of the progeny were incredibly nervous, one or two were anything but timid, and on the subject of timid wolf hybrids a few reported crosses in Eastern Europe and tales of Clarke's researches into dangerous dog/wolf hybrids made the sale of these pups a thing of questionable legality. If the Beasts of Gevaudan or the tale of Courtaud was anything to go by, chances are that my quaint old lady, who had not only unknowingly donated her loving pet for my experiment, but every Christmas had presented me with quantities of rhubarb wine, might achieve a somewhat doubtful reputation as a dog breeder. I had visions of a once happily married couple from Armitage telling their friends 'Don't go to that Mrs Saunders for a puppy, the one we had from her ate our David!' Still, Naylor with some trepidation agreed to allow my neighbour's bitch a chance of being served by a wolf and seemed more worried about whether she had been inoculated for distemper and leptospirosis than as to whether his wolf would eat her.

'What will you do if your wolf attacks my dog?' I asked somewhat cautiously. 'Dunno,' replied Naylor, 'what will you do if your dog attacks my wolf?' Gazing down at Suki, the fat, waddling, over-eager bitch at my feet I couldn't but help wonder what the devil Naylor meant by his comment and for the hell of me I couldn't stop myself wondering what rhymed with Suki, if in the event of an accident I had to write an elegy for the poor devil. For the first time during the whole experiment I had doubts as to whether what I was doing was morally right.

Naylor snapped me out of my reverie. 'Are you sure she is ready to stand for the mating? The twelfth day is usually about the right time.' Quite suddenly for no reason in particular I began to speculate about whether Shakespeare had any ulterior motive in calling one of his plays *Twelfth Night*, but was snapped back to reality by a nudge from Naylor who was observing Suki's attitude towards the great drim dweller of the northern plains. Suki was pushing her buttocks against the bars of the cage turning her tail aside in the manner of a French can-can dancer who was about to be fired for indecency. 'Yes, I think she is ready', Naylor remarked, and began to unlock the cage which held the Siberian grey. Suki needed no urging and flung herself through the opening at her stately, but come to think of it, reluctant, lover.

Things didn't go to plan from this time onwards if I remember correctly, with Suki dashing around the cage thrusting her derrière at the bewildered wolf who snarled, spat, moved away from her and finally finished up grovelling in the corner as if pleading to join his two staid and respectable wives and escape from this exasperating nymphomaniac. How man misuses the wolf in present day English usage! A 'wolf' is a term applied to a man who is successful at seducing women; a 'wolf whistle' is a sharp two-noted cry of appreciation from a supposedly virile man; and the French term 'she has seen the wolf' is applied to a woman who has just been deflowered by a vigorous rake. I gazed at the fake, cringing in the corner, covering his face with a paw like a gauche schoolboy trying to avoid his classmates noticing his blushes. Man had maligned the wolf – and brother, I mean maligned.

Needless to say Suki did not conceive and returned her *virgo intacta* and with all four legs to old Mrs Saunders, stating that my friend's alsatian was not interested in mating her – and thereby, I must add, allowing Mrs Saunders to remain a well-respected member of the community, and the population of Armitage to remain uneaten. Still, it didn't stop my interest in trying to breed or own and train a wolf/dog hybrid. At one time I followed up every reported case of dog/fox mating – none of the supposed progeny of which proved to be the real McCoy. Now I began to investigate every reported case of a dog/wolf litter, and brother, oh brother, aren't there some strange people in this world; and I fear I've met most of them. Once I chanced upon an advert, in a well-known paper I must add; which stated 'alsatian cross wolf cross-bred £25'. I raced to the phone booth in the village, dialled the number and breathlessly enquired about the puppies or cubs, call them what you will. 'Yeh,' said a broad Liverpudlian accent, 'my bitch got out and was mated by a stray wolf.' As the chap lived in Salford (a suburb of Manchester) at the time I believe, his tale didn't sound all that convincing, but you never can tell with Manchester, I suppose.

Then one day, to use an Americanism, I got lucky. At least I got lucky regarding a true report, an authentic case of a dog/wolf hybrid. Breeding wolves for films is big business in the Eastern Bloc countries for few Russian-made films don't have scenes concerning wolves attacking a happy troika-carried party of Ruskies, with the revellers finally forced to sacrifice the horses to the wolves, and finally finishing up the night beneath the sleigh, burning pieces of the vehicle to keep the wolves away. This sort of scene is a 'must' for every Russian film.

In fact the only reason the Russians don't go in for science fiction type films is that the sight of packs of hungry wolves attacking a space rocket would look just a bit out of place. Well, to fake a shot of starving wolves attacking men and horses alike would take some doing as wolves are a timid bunch regarding attacking to order, and even the slap of a clapperboard is often enough to panic a whole grey bunch of them. So the stage props people got their heads together and contacted a group of big-game hunters called the Sigethy brothers who owned a ranch-sized farm in a place called Göndöllö in Hungary (no, I don't know what the dots mean either). Both brothers agreed that to control a pack of pure-bred wolves well enough to play out the attack sequence was impossible, but somehow they managed to produce a cross-bred litter of wolf/alsatian hybrids which looked real enough to fool the public and a little too real for the actors' liking. The hybrids were fiendishly vicious with golden fawn legs and chest and a wolf-like head. Their dog heritage made them unafraid of man and their wolf blood gave them the necessary 'go' to follow up this lack of fear. Tale has it the Sigethy brothers wouldn't go into the compound with their hybrids without a stick, gun or heavy whip. If they had the Sigethy brothers might have become the Sigethy brother. Well Göndöllö was a long way away so I suppose I just had to take the Sigethy brothers' word for it, but just three weeks later I really did get lucky. One day I received a letter from a chap in Leamington Spa who had read of my interest in wolves in my book *Diary of A Hunter* (buy it folks don't get it from the library, financially things are not going too well lately). Well, to cut a long story short he mentioned that a chap called Raymond Graham-Jones, the owner of a zoo in Southam, a tiny village near Leamington Spa, had bred a litter of wolf/dog hybrids using a large grey timber wolf male and a rather elderly alsatian. I'm always a bit sceptical about supposed hybrids of this sort bred from alsatian females, as the German Shepherd Dog looks a bit like a wolf anyway, but on the off-chance I phoned Graham-Jones and arranged for a visit.

He turned out to be a delightful eccentric, a joy to listen to, the sort of chap who could tell animal tales for a week non-stop and still be totally fascinating. He began my introduction into his world by insisting I played with his tame leopard and his almost tame jaguars and tigers, and though I suggested I should start with the wallabies and work up, and that I was 'only there for the wolves' he wouldn't hear of it and dragged me into enclosure after enclosure full of the sort of creatures which readily see off all of Tarzan's enemies in vintage Johnny Weismüller films. That horrifying experience over, he introduced me to the sire and dam of the puppies/cubs, a very tame timber wolf with a penchant for ice-cream and a tired old alsatian bitch. I looked at the cubs and realised they were the real McCoy, golden legs and chest, wolf-like eyes and shape, exact replicas of the Beasts of Gevaudan, the bobtailed Courtaud, and the sleigh-attacking pets of the Sigethy brothers. One had been sold to Canada, the second to Scotland, and Graham-Jones was keeping the three bitches. As I left Southam I watched Graham-Jones sharing his raspberry ripple with the denizen of the darkness, and got to thinking man has given the wolf a hell of a bad time over these last several thousand years.

Harassed, butchered and persecuted, just about summarises man's treatment of good old *Canis Lupus Linaeus* and his cousins. No method of destroying him seems to be too grisly to perpetuate. One of the nastiest methods of seeing off wolves is the one used by certain Eskimo tribes who live in Northern Canada (and from the inhuman way they treat wolves I'm sure glad they live in Canada and not Lichfield). Eskimos troubled by wolves raiding their caches of whale blubber and other unpleasant Eskimo delicacies, would bend a piece of whalebone double and tie it with some animal sinew. This curious little device was placed in a ball of tallow and left on the ice for a prowling *Canis Lupus Lineaus* or any other beast unfortunate enough to find it. Wolves swallowed these balls whole and after the stomach juices had dissolved the tallow and etched their way into the sinew, the whalebone spring exploded, springing open, tearing into the stomach walls leaving the poor devil to die an agonising death from peritonitis. Really I don't like people all that much and Eskimos, Nell aside, certainly don't come top of my popularity list people-wise.

Neither do Europeans for that matter, for we as a race seem to have gone out of our way to not only see off the wolf, but to make the manner of his demise as unpleasant as possible. In alpine regions a small yellow-flowered plant called the Aconite is found. Its other name is wolf bane and at this point I think I'd best explain the word 'bane'. Bane means a murderer or a destroyer, so the word prefaced by some unfortunate animal's name means it doesn't do much good to the beast in question. Hence rat bane quickly polishes off rats and hen bane doesn't do poultry a lot of good either. Aconite was called wolf bane because the juice of the flower smeared on lumps of meat and left in places where wolves fed caused the wolves to die an unpleasant death, staggering and tottering into unconsciousness over a matter of days. Fortunately we are more civilised these days and now wolf-poisoners use strychnine, a substance which when ingested by wolves causes intense agony and sends the beast into such convulsions that they dislocate their own jaws, and the poison causes the body to become contorted and rigid, so horrifyingly painful is the manner of the victim's death. Yes, we've progressed a lot since the Middle Ages.

Well, quite a spell before the Middle Ages, about a thousand years before Christ actually, a race called the Celts who lived in Southern Russia began to think about migrating across Europe for some reason or other. With them they took sheep, cattle, pigs and a curious looking water dog bred for fetching shot ducks and geese off lakes and rivers. We call this breed of dog the poodle today, but what fascinated the Romans who witnessed and suffered from this migration was the sight of enormous dogs the size of a small pony, dogs capable of killing a man and doing a fairly unpleasant job on a wolf or a boar. Today we call the descendants of these dogs Irish Wolf-Hounds and Scottish Deer-Hounds, typey elegant dogs more at home in the halls of some Scottish laird than in the show-ring at Crufts. The original dogs were a damned sight more impressive so the tale goes. About ten years ago a farmer's plough turned up a skull of a dog in a recently drained piece of land that had once been an Irish peat bog. The skull was enormous and scientists have gauged that if the rest of this dog's anatomy matched the skull the monster must have measured four feet at the shoulder. Four feet, a colossus of a dog, more the size of a donkey than a dog; but such dogs were valued as much for their courage as their size, and the traditional quarry of these brutes was the wolf.

Kings gave fellow kings gifts of these magnificent hounds, the most famous of which was the legendary Gelert, the giant wolf-hound supposedly given by King John to Llewellyn, a North Welsh prince. Forget the idea of princes of this time living in Gothic 'Snow White' type castles and dressing like extras from the *Prisoner of Zenda*; Llewellyn lived, so the tale goes, in a wattle and daub two-roomed shack, as did most of the Welsh princes of the time. Anyway accommodation aside, Llewellyn was a mighty hunter and did a fair job of denuding North Wales of large game such as wolves, bears, boars and deer. One day however, he whistled up his pack for another day's carnage and found Gelert reluctant to leave the hovel, which incidentally housed Llewellyn's heir to the throne, a baby of maybe eight or nine months of age. In spite of warnings from shepherds, wood-cutters and sundries who in the very best of folk legends are the only ones credited with any brain at all, Llewellyn disregarded their tales that wolf-hounds are more than just keen on enjoying a hearty snack of an odd infant or so and decided to leave the hound in charge of the child. Well, without his trusty hound in tow the hunt proved something of a flop, and Llewellyn, denied his right to cripple and slay any stray animal, came home in a bad humour. On returning to the hovel Llewellyn found the house in disarray, chairs torn, tables overturned, the place smashed to pieces, looking a little like the church hall which staged *As You Like It* and allowed in a crowd of skinheads who mistook the gig for a discotheque. The walls of the hovel were spattered with blood and Llewellyn realised he should have heeded the shepherds', or was it the wood-cutters' warning. Suddenly, up leaps Gelert to greet Llewellyn, the hound's mouth awash with blood. Llewellyn goes berserk at this point and stabs the huge hound through the heart to avenge his dead and probably eaten child. Suddenly there is a cry from the other room of the two-down-no-up shack and Llewellyn races in to find his child beneath a pile of blankets and a huge wolf, throat torn asunder, dead in the corner; Llewellyn true to form bursts into tears and erects a huge mound of stones to commemorate the grave of his faithful hound, and calls the spot 'Beth Gelert', the place of Gelert. The tale is a real tear-jerker and once when I had the misfortune to teach Lower Juniors (aged 7–8) in Rotherham I used the tale often at the end of the day and there wasn't a dry eye in the house. In fact if the kids played up during sums or the dreaded comprehension, I took my revenge on the little sods by giving them another dose of Gelert – day in day out until I broke them. Funnily enough the head didn't give me a reference when I left that school, and after the number of tears each and every delinquent teeny shed, I didn't have the heart to tell them the whole story was a fraud.

Fraud it is I'm afraid – although even the creation of the lie is a good tale. In 1793 a Welshman called David Pritchard became landlord of an inn called the Royal Goat (there's a reason for inn names so I'm told) and things weren't going too well for the place and the town which was called at that time Beth Kelert (Kelert was the name of a Welsh saint, of which there are so I believe 100,000,000). Well, Pritchard needed to drum up some trade and fast, so quick as a flash he invents the story, calls the hound Gelert, builds a mound of rocks over the body of a dead collie and in weeks the place was thronged with sight-seeing tourists. A happy ending to the story though kind of rough on collies I've always thought. Well I'd laughed and laughed over the con-trick I'd pulled on those weeping teenies (I'm not a very nice person really) when one day I picked up a book written by a chap called Cadog the Wise (there aren't many of those in Wales, saints yes, 'wise' no). The book had been written in the fifth century and contained an almost identical tale, and ended with a proverb which says 'I'm as sad as the man who slew his greyhound'.

Funnily enough by the twelfth century there weren't all that many wolves in Britain, as they'd been just about hunted to extinction by that time, though they were the very devil to hunt, for the task of killing them required numerous dogs and a great number of beaters.

In fact so tedious was the task of hunting down lamb- and sheep-killing wolves the Anglo Saxon kings sentenced criminals to hunt wolves as a punishment – a little like the Saturday punishment centres for football rowdies I've always thought. Some Welsh princes actually paid their taxes to Saxon overlords in wolf pelts, though in 940 AD one prince failed to pay as he claimed the wolf was extinct in Wales.

Not everyone found the hunting of wolves a chore however, In 1887 a Russian archduke with the unpronounceable name of Nicolai Nikolajawitsch founded the Perchino Kennel of Borzois, long thin elegant Russian wolf-hounds. Fox-hounds would drive wolves from the forest and a trio of these Perchino of Borzois would be slipped on the hapless wolf which was bowled and held by the hounds, whereupon huntsmen would rush up and bind the wolf's muzzle wedging a wooden stake between its teeth, and the wolf so bound and muzzled was taken back to the forest and released. A pointless activity if you ask me and I can understand why the Bolsheviks rose up and overthrew such aristrocratic nutters.

But for the most spectacular form of wolf killing and probably the most barbaric as well if one discounts traps and the Eskimos' whalebone trick, you'd go a long way to beat the method designed by a Central Asian tribe called the Khirgiz. These people did considerable trade in wolf skins and being as the trotting gait of a wolf tires out almost any breed of dog, in order to get a suitable pelt for selling and also to get pelts in number they fly a very large dark golden eagle called the Kholsan or Berkute at the wolf. In order to fly wolf, an unnatural quarry for any eagle – they starve their eagles to the point where if the eagle misses the wolf and has to return to the falconer's fist it's every man for himself with the eagle attacking dogs, horses or men at random. To train eagles to fly such enormous and ferocious animals is quite a task and is usually accomplished by flying a young eagle at a stuffed wolf, from the eye sockets of which are hung long thin shreds of meat. Once the eagle had become first-rate at stopping the stuffed wolf which was dragged behind a horse, and the bird had learned to bind to the wolf's carcass with feet on its throat and loin – a stance which prevented retaliation from the wolf – the eagle was taken out and flown at live wolves, and eagles being the D-streamers of the bird kingdom immediately thought that the creature running below it had slivers of goodies hanging from its eyes. Down would flash the eagle dealing the wolf a savage blow across the eyes, toppling it, pinning it in the throat/loin hold and delaying it long enough for the Khirgiz falconer to come up on the battlers and despatch the wolf with a spear. A spectacle designed to enthral the viewer and make him get down on his knees and thank God that he wasn't born a wolf, but for real weirdo stuff the Khirgiz couldn't hold a candle to a retired German cavalry officer called F. W. Remmler.

Remmler and I had two things in common, one his passion for the chase and the second that he seemed none too struck on children. He trained eagles to hunt wolves in Finland in 1930 much in the manner of the Khirgiz of Central Asia; the difference was in the manner Remmler trained his birds, for he started them on children dressed in leather and wolf skins with meat strapped to their backs. The eagles were then trained to attack the wolf/children. I suggested this activity to a head master of mine a few years ago as a sports afternoon with a difference for a very difficult 5K I once taught, but the head wouldn't 'wear it' – something to do with unions not backing the idea I think he said.

On the subject of wolf/children, see preceding paragraph, which I think brings us very cleverly on to the next part of this schpiel. Stories of wolves adopting children are a dime a dozen not only in England and Asia, but also in the New World, and many of these tales seem a little more than incredible when one gets to grips with the facts. Not all tales of animals adopting children bear up to examination, mind you. In 1948 an amazing story came out of India, concerning a young antelope boy reputedly running with a small family of black buck, a type of antelope which vies with the cheetah as being the fastest creature in the animal kingdom. The tale was that a party of hunters had seen the naked lad, a youth aged maybe ten or so, feeding on grass and browsing on bushes in a scrubland area in Northern India. The hunters had slipped some greyhounds on the black buck and boy combo, but both antelopes and child outstripped the greyhounds. Now I was eleven at the time, and even at that age I could see that anyone who believed a boy could outrun a brace of greyhounds not only had a proverbial tile missing, but actually was in receipt of a considerable amount of water rushing in. Yet strangely enough the adult population of the world went wild about this boy and nearly every major newspaper covered the tale. A year later nearly every sensation-seeking journalist had egg on his face, for the whole story exploded as a ridiculous hoax set up by a visiting film crew who 'bought' a mentally defective boy and encouraged the poor devil to dine on grass and browse on bushes. Hold on to the mentally defective bit a moment though, we'll be back to that in a page or so.

Of course the most famous story of wolves adopting children is the great oldy of Romulus and Remus, the architects and builders of ancient Rome, who were supposedly found in the forest by a she-wolf and suckled by her long enough to survive until a shepherd had a chance to rescue them and rear them. Wartime Italian stamps often showed a bronze statue of a she-wolf, heavy with milk, suckling two small infants. Plutarch gives a lengthy account of the tale and here things start to get just a shade out of kilter. The Latin for a she-wolf is *lupa*. *Lupa* is also the slang term used by Roman legionaries for a prostitute, much in the same way that modern criminal running slang dubs such ladies tarts, whores or whatever you care to think of. So did Plutarch somehow get it all wrong and were the founders of Rome found by a prostitute rather than a she-wolf and reared in a bordello rather than a wild wood?

India abounds with tales of wolves adopting children and there was a spate of these tales in the 1880s which may or may not have inspired Kipling to write his fascinating *Jungle Book* in 1894. In this book some wolves find a tiny infant whose mother had lost him in the forest and the boy whom the wolves somehow manage to name Mowgli (which means frog – hardly complimentary) is adopted, reared and educated by wolves, pythons, panthers and monkeys (I've worked in some residential schools where the staff were also pretty strange). Mowgli grows into a normal healthy little chap, a bit keen on blood for some mothers, but able to enter into the world of men when he is ready for the change, and although he finds man's perfidy and odd behaviour a bit disconcerting he is easily able to integrate into village life and adapt to the ways of men. In point of fact children who have supposedly been reared by animals don't fare so well when do-gooders try to civilise them.

Rousseau, whose ideas on education bored me to death in training college, was quite convinced wolves did steal and rear human babies and wrote in some length about a rather unpleasantly maladjusted wolf-child of Hesse who turned up in 1344 and behaved like a ravening wild dog. Linnaeus, who gave the animals and plants of this planet those curious Latin names which allow scientists the world over to understand each other, but kills the average man's interest in biology stone-dead, studied forty such children and put them in a class apart from normal man calling them *Homo Ferus* (wild man), but there are some reasonably well authenticated cases of supposedly (and I use the word with my tongue firmly in my cheek) normal children being adopted and reared by wolves.

The tale that causes me most concern is that of the so-called Dent child who was reputedly the child of Mollie and John Dent and born in 1835. Mollie Dent died in childbirth in a cabin in Devils River in Texas and John Dent was killed in a thunderstorm when he was riding for help for his 'in labour' wife. Help did arrive but the child was never found and because the area around the Dent homestead was heavily padded with wolf prints, the locals believed that the child had been devoured by wolves which infested the Del Rio area at that time.

However ten years later a young shepherd boy living near Del Rio brought back a terrifying tale of an attack by wolves on his flock of sheep and goats. Running among the wolves and taking a very active part in the carnage was a creature which the boy stated could have been a young girl. At first no one seems to have believed the boy – and frankly who could blame them – but quite suddenly several Apache scouts reported having seen a child running with wolves and there were cases of human footprints found among wolf pad marks near many ranches. Subsequently the locals, in the worst possible taste I think, planned a hunt for the child.

The hunt lasted some three days and eventually the posse cornered the terrified child in a canyon in the company of a young wolf. The wolf was shot and the child, who manifested all the behaviour of a frightened wolf, captured with nets and lariat. Not surprisingly she was terrified by the experience, but she was later bound and taken to a nearby ranch and released in an enclosed room the windows of which were shuttered and the door locked.

During the daylight hours the child huddled in a corner in a characteristic monkey ball shape, but as the night approached she became more lively, howling, baying and pawing the walls of the cabin. Her cries attracted numerous wolves to the ranch and the presence of these wolves 'spooked' the stock, allowing the girl to escape in the ensuing melée. She was neither seen nor was any report of the child made until 1852 when a surveying crew saw her cavorting and playing with two wolf cubs on a sandbar on the Rio Grande, after which in the manner of the very best fairy stories she was never seen again.

Far-fetched, heavily embroidered? Well, perhaps, but the next tale has been a little more than just authenticated by hearsay. India can boast a wealth of stories concerning wolves adopting and rearing children, the most famous of which is the tale of the wolf girls of Godamuri, a town some miles from Calcutta. In 1920 a Sikh clergyman, the Revd J. A. L. Singh, was running an orphanage at Mindapore. Part of his duties however involved safari type expeditions to convert to Christianity various aboriginal tribes which lived in remote jungles some two hundred miles north of Calcutta. It was an interesting if exhausting task and Singh encountered many curious superstitions and tales of devils and ghosts among the primitive tribesmen of that area. One particular so-called 'ghost man' seemed to terrify the natives and Singh, who considered it his Christian duty to dispel superstition, set out to investigate the phenomenon.

Supposedly this ghost man, a troll-sized hairy beast running on all fours, lived in a wolf lair in a hole in one of those disused ant-hills which abound in Northern India. Singh set up a platform in a nearby tree and set watch. He didn't have long to wait. At dusk on October 9th 1920 he saw two fully-grown Indian wolves (collie-sized beasts of a slightly different species from our own European wolves) emerge from the lair followed by cubs. Moments later a monstrous troll-like creature covered in filth and its head a mass of matted hair and plastered mud crept out of the lair. Even Singh who was an educated man not given to believing in natives' superstitions was more than a little alarmed, as the eyes of the creature glowed with an almost unnatural brightness. Singh concluded that the creature was human or close to human, and when a smaller beast, similar in type, followed the first ghost man out of the lair, Singh reported the facts to the village head man and a 'dig' was organised.

As the diggers began to excavate the lair a small female wolf emerged from time to time and attacked the diggers before vanishing into the deeper recesses of the wolf den. These attacks became more and more frequent as the diggers went deeper into the mound and finally the diggers were forced to shoot her. Excavation continued until finally the diggers broke through the walls of the central chamber only to find two wolf cubs curled up with two terrified naked girl children, one aged, so Singh says, roughly eighteen months or so and the other a few years older. Somehow the Rev Singh seems to have lost control of his diggers at this point for both wolf cubs and children, who bit, scratched and snarled with equal ferocity, were crated up by the Indian workmen and offered for sale in the market place in Godamuri. Both children were kept in a tiny cage in which neither could stand up even if they wished to (for both ran on all fours in the manner of a dog and seemed reluctant to walk upright). After two weeks the man in charge of them abandoned the pair and Singh received the two feral girls at his orphange, caked in their own filth and half starved.

The younger child, Singh called her Amala, did not thrive in captivity and died a year later. The older child, Kamala, lived to maybe seventeen years of age before dying of uremic poisoning. At first, light hurt the children's eyes and they tended to become active only after sunset, and both children had eyes which glowed when a strong light was shone on them. When upset, disturbed or made angry they bit like dogs, preferring to eat alongside Singh's pet fox-terrier. Carrion was the favourite diet of Kamala and she seemed to be able to track pieces of meat which Singh left around the orphanage grounds with the enthusiasm of a good hound.

Singh never quite managed to break the girls of the habit of howling by night, and neither child learned to master human speech. One of the most fascinating features of both children, in my opinion anyway, is the fact that neither child seemed to mind heat or cold and neither perspired during the time they spent at the orphange. Linnaeus (just jump back a few pages) who studied forty cases of such children was convinced that people who displayed these tendencies, and quite a few of Linnaeus' 'cases' didn't perspire, were not quite human. It is also worth noting that neither dogs nor wolves perspire and lose heat simply by a panting action as did Amala and Kamala.

Most people regarded Singh, who kept a day-by-day diary of the lives of both children, as at the best a first-rate spinner of the type of yarn popular in the 1920s, and at the worst a liar, and his amazing story became forgotten until about 1940 when a Yale professor of child development called Arnold Gesell (who was unique among psychologists as he could write a sentence which other people could understand) examined Singh's account and pronounced it genuine. He also said he had no doubt Amala and Kamala had been reared by wolves up until the time they were dug out of the ant-hill.

Hold on a moment though, and a quick flashback to the success-studded life of one D. B. Plummer who when the education authorities had begun to realise that he wasn't of any use lecturing in a university or training college, or teaching in a secondary modern or junior school, tactfully suggested he might try a spell teaching (if that's the right word) autistic children. So dictionary out and at the ready I looked up the word autistic and did a quick check up on the little habits of the same. Webster's Dictionary, at least my shop-soiled copy £1.75 page 734 missing, says that autistics are 'absorbed in fantasy and introspection to the exclusion of interest in objective reality' which didn't mean much to me either, so I pressed on regardless and started enquiring into what exactly Webster – who must have had an amazing vocabulary if his book is anything to go by – meant by autistic, and forthwith I dropped on an account of an experiment conducted in the 1950s at the Sonia Shankman Institute in Chicago, where psychologists (the word means something a shade different in America) were conducting research into the treatment of some nineteen rather unusual children. These children were dormant by day becoming alive at night, building dens from rubbish and smashed furniture and eating for preference raw and bloody meat. Some of these ran about on all fours, licked blocks of salt for hours at a time and one attacked a nurse with her teeth doing about the same damage as would an enraged bull terrier. Not one had been in contact with a wolf and all were from middle-class Chicago backgrounds. Needless to say I did not apply for a job teaching autistic children, a job which would have scared the hell out of me, and spent the next nine months working on the motorway – that bit just south of Leicester to be exact – but it did set me thinking of Amala, Kamala, the wolf children of Hesse and some of Linnaeus' case-histories. Were these children simply mimicking the habits of their wolf foster-parents or were the children born autistic and caused their parents such concern that rather than put a pillow over the face of the child, a once common practice in breadline Indian families when such families realised their kids were peculiar, they abandoned them in the forest? Would Amala and Kamala have behaved any differently if they had been reared in a normal household? Were they sisters who, when their parents realised they'd bred two autistic children rather than one, were thrown out to fend for themselves, and as autistics are often drawn to stroking puppies and kittens, did they crawl into the lair and get accepted by the she-wolf who considered them no harm to her cubs? Unlikely perhaps and personally I can't see it, but neither myself nor any authority concerning these strange cases can come up with another more convincing explanation.

Running on all fours, baying at night, eating raw flesh – one step further and I hate to say it and you have a quaint old Gothic horror creature beloved by pre-war film producers – the werewolf. Now not only gone-out loonies believe in werewolves – though I admit the man in the street probably never gives them a second thought. Some years ago I had the good fortune to meet a gentleman called the Revd Montague Summers, a shrill-voiced clergyman who not only was acknowledged as being an expert on werewolves and bedfellows (there's a macabre statement for you mate, 'bedfellows') but he also scared the pants off them. Summers' little classics *The Vampire in Europe*, *The Werewolf* and a few other grisly epics don't exactly make recommended reading for the nervous, the easily upset or those likely to be alone in the house at night, but they certainly set one thinking about what in hell could have started up the numerous legends concerning werewolves, for Montague Summers was a chap who really knew his lycanthropy (see Webster's shop-soiled edition page 841 starting with 'lustful').

My bet is that all these cases of werewolves and allied friends of the night could all be attributed to cases of severely autistic people with some physical peculiarities – I'll come back to that later – although once, when I was attempting to make a not-so-fast-buck translating books of spells for enthusiastic would-be witches, warlocks and near-lunatics, I came upon a spell and a potion which when used in conjunction with the full moon could turn a man into a werewolf (admittedly it didn't offer a money-back guarantee, but then people were a bit sloppy about the Trades Descriptions Act's regulations in the Middle Ages).

The potion – which contained such goodies as hen bane, opium poppy and hemlock – was boiled in a pot with the fat of a young child and wood soot (I really fancied the young child bit as I'd had a bad time at school that week, but the spell offered a substitute, namely vegetable oil, which is more easily obtainable and less likely to cause concern in the district where I live). While this is boiling one should repeat a strange chant concerning wolves, spirits of the night (stamped addressed envelopes please) and a few other less pleasant things and then the ointment is applied to one's body when the 'yucky' has cooled somewhat, chanting the spell while striking one's head on the ground three times. Well, one evening when I was at my wits' end for something interesting to do and the telly had packed up, I decided to chance getting shot for sheep-worrying and have a crack at seeing whether any of these spells actually worked. I suppose I must have got the mix wrong or perhaps I was a little too enthusiastic about the striking of my head three times on the ground as all I got out of it was diarrhoea (page 390 Webster's) and a blinding headache, but it helped to pass the time until the telly was repaired I suppose.

On the subject of the werewolf's appearance – its hairy face and ears – there's a very rare disease called Hypertrichosia Universalis Congenita which is so uncommon that there's no reference to it in my copy of Webster's. The victim of this complaint has long hair which grows all over the body excepting on the palms of the hand and the soles of the feet and white bristly hair seems to grow out of the ears. Hang on, may be it's the hypochondria I've inherited from Mam, but that bit about the long bristly hair growing out of the ears – I'm sure I've got that disorder. I'll just check in the mirror a moment – My God – I can't see my reflection!

ANIMAL LOVERS-
84

—7—

A Nation of Animal Lovers?

I SUPPOSE KIPLING is to blame for giving the rest of the world the notion that we are a nation of animal lovers, and that the average Britisher is simply nuts about dogs in particular, and animals in general. Remember his poem 'The Power Of The Dog', an emotion-packed little epic which culminates in the tear-jerking line 'Brothers and sisters, I bid you beware of giving your heart to a dog to tear' – not literally of course, Rudyard for all his dying for one's country jazz had sense enough to stay well away from the macabre. The continentals, from the Calais-born Frog to the most Easterly Ural-born Rusky believe that to a man we are more concerned about the welfare of our animals than we are about our children, and it's a fact that the average 2.4-kids Britisher spends more on pet food than he does on baby food, which with my natural antipathy towards children I can understand perfectly well. However, to call the British a nation of animal lovers is stretching the truth just a shade, particularly if one considers our track record concerning cruelty to animals.

Still, the continentals really believe that we are, to use a good old Romany expression 'animal daft', and anyone who has travelled abroad knows that when a Britisher buys a house in France or Spain, the natives automatically expect him to stock up the place with hordes of large hairy dogs and a variety of unpleasant 'critters' which would cause the average Kraut housewife to have a convulsion should one of her children so much as bring one over the doorstep. Try hitch-hiking in Germany folks and once you accept an act of charity from a German car driver you will really get to know what the average German thinks of us as a nation. Some twenty years ago I used to hitch-hike quite a lot and bum around the continent, hoping and day-dreaming that a swish sports car driven by a Britt Ekland type fraulein or frau – I've never been fussy – would pull up and literally drag me into the car pleading for me to accept a lift. It never happened of course, but I met a variety of strange people which proved to me it's not only the British who are a trifle odd.

Take for instance the lift I had twixt Munchengladbach and Luneberg, and I'll get to the point of the story in seconds. I put my thumb up, a car flashed past me, I shouted something unspeakable and found another car slithered to a halt and a small black-haired Austrian, a sort of Ira Levin type clone of 'you know who' opened the door of the car and invited me in. In no time at all we were on to the shortcomings of the British. We kicked off with the usual epithets concerning us Pommies or whatever the Krauts call us, you know – lazy, shiftless, strike-orientated, over indulgent – and I closed my eyes for I knew what was going to follow 'you're so schtupid about animals'. Now let's get it right: no one, but no one could ever accuse an Austrian of being over-sentimental about animals, not according to a certain Dr Charles Burney who visited Austria in 1772 and was so upset about what he saw that he raced back home to England and promptly dashed off a nasty little diatribe about anything other than British, called *Continental Travels*. Well, the climax of Dr Charles' trip to the continent was a Sunday visit to Vienna, which far from being a city of Strauss type waltzes was a fairly nasty place for an animal to live, if live is the correct word. A passing Viennese thrust a handbill of that Sunday's entertainments into poor old Burney's hands and the events advertised therein turned the doctor green. The handbill read as follows (the italics are my comments but the rest is true and accurate).

'This day by Imperial Licence in the Great Amphitheatre at five o'clock will begin the following diversions:

1st: A wild Hungarian Ox in full fire (*which incidentally means an ox with bundles of burning straw tied to its horns, its genitals and pushed up its anus, plus a few lighted fireworks put in selected places*) will be set on by dogs.'

A show stopper by any standards and as if this wasn't enough, course two consisted of:

'2nd: A wild boar in the same manner (*which means I suspect also full of fire*) will be baited by dogs.' And just in case the audience had tired of blazing, agonised beasts the theme changes slightly.

'3rd: A great bear will be immediately torn apart by dogs (*which I suppose makes a change*).

4th: A wolf will be hunted by dogs of the fleetest kind (*which were fairly sure of catching the wolf as the whole affair took place in an enclosed amphitheatre*).

5th: A very furious and enraged wild bull from Hungary (*he'd probably seen Act I and had cause to be enraged*) will be attacked by fierce and hungry dogs.

6th: A fresh, wild bear (*clearly not the one from Act III if the show went as expected*) will be attacked by hounds.

7th: Will appear a fierce wild boar just caught which will now be baited by dogs defended by armour (*clearly the Austrians were a bit soft about dogs*).

8th: A furious and hungry bear which has had no food for several days will attack a young bull and eat him alive, and if he (*the bear I suppose*) is unable to finish the job a wolf will be ready to help him (*though I doubt after several days hunger a bear would need much help*).'

Now good old Doctor Burney was a little shocked about the whole messy business and wrote of it 'hardly fit for a civilised and polished nation to allow', but the Hun and his fun aside, messy and brutal as such a spectacle must have appeared, things were none too pleasant for beasts in Britain either at that time.

Now it can be said that Britain didn't put on tortures on such a grand scale, but only because the British pursued such large creatures as boars, bears and wild oxen with such fury that they had ceased to exist in Britain by the twelfth or thirteenth century. However we still had a host of smaller animals, both tame and wild, and these were certainly worthy of our consideration. Take for instance the cutest little pastime which started up halfway through the eighteenth century and was still going strong as late as 1860. In 1748 a Kildare man (not that he was Irish explains anything, mind you) performing at Tregonwall Frampton, set up five live fox cubs and scoffed the lot, tails as well, in front of an astonished crowd. However this was nothing compared to the feat of a shepherd from Beverley, Yorkshire who turned up at a country fair with a large, live, black tom-cat and, for a bet of a guinea, proceeded to devour the terrified beast alive, finishing off the last morsel in a quarter of an hour. Now it would seem just a little unlikely that an activity like cat-eating would catch on, but if the reader can remember the same was said of glue-sniffing. Cat-eating caught on like wildfire, partly due to the good auspices of the Barrymore family, as neat a band of weirdos as ever graced an upper-class household. So crazy were the Barrymores that their friends called the brothers Hellgate, Cripplegate and Newgate respectively, naming the brothers after the gallows spots of the city of London. The oldest brother was fascinated with the tale of the Beverley shepherd and bet the Duke of Bedford, another fiend, who disbelieved the tale of the Yorkshire feline-eater, that such a deed was possible, and after scouting around the countryside for a suitable lunatic he came upon one in the town of Harpenden who in 1788 ate cats by the score, thus winning Barrymore's bet with the Duke of Bedford. Apart from the hideous cruelty involved in eating a live cat, it really must have been quite a feat to devour a terrified feline which would certainly make incredibly good use of its teeth and worse still its claws.

Cat-eating was, however, a spot of cruelty confined only to the lower class, while those with a little more money simply went out and crimped a salmon. Salmon have always been quite expensive fish to serve at a meal, partly due to the exquisite taste of the 'meat' and partly due to its wonderously attractive colour, a colour which reverts to a dirty whitish shade when the fish goes off a little; so gourmets usually crimped up the salmon alive, chopping it to manageable steaks while the wretched creature flopped and floundered on the slab. Of course this little pursuit was abolished some time ago, but lobsters, and boy, don't the upper-class gourmets go for bright pinky-orange food, are still killed by dropping them into boiling water, which doesn't exactly please the lobster very much but allows it to stay 'in the pink' as the saying goes. Anglers however, in an effort to preserve their sport, no doubt, state that the Almighty in his wisdom didn't give fish any feelings, and perhaps a fish actually does enjoy getting hooked time and time again, but somehow I just don't feel a salmon gets much of a thrill out of being 'crimped'.

Fish may or may not have a great deal of 'feeling' but pigs almost certainly do, which brings us to that rather exclusively British pastime of pig-whipping – no, you've not made a mistake – pig-whipping. Now and again we see TV chefs pounding pieces of steak with mallets to tenderise the meat – which it does, as the cell structure of the meat is broken down by the repeated smashing action of the mallet. Now during the eighteenth and nineteenth centuries pork was also tenderised by smashing the cell structure, by beating it with a knotted rope, the difference being of course that eighteenth-century lovers of good food didn't bother to kill the pig first and dealt the poor devil blow after blow with a knotted rope until the porker was simply pulverised alive, if alive is the correct word. Shocked, dear reader? Well, just for the book, pigs were still being done to death or tenderised, call it what you will, as late as 1900 to please the die-hard diner who liked his pork really juicy and tender. Pigs are quite sensitive animals – I've taught a few – and die with child-like screams even when killed humanely by the electricity-charged 'ear-phone' contraptions found at modern abattoirs; whipped to death they would have bleated pitifully before expiring and it must have been a callous fiend who could continue to beat a pig to death. Pope, the poet, wrote to the

Guardian in 1773 to state how much he disliked pig-whipping. The pigs didn't care for it much either.

When one thinks of it, amazing horrors have been perpetrated on animals just to produce a meal to tickle the most sensitive palate, simply because prior to Victorian times folk didn't believe animals had souls, and a person so inclined could hack a slice and chop pieces of any animal without fear of eternal damnation. Thus in addition to salmon crimping, turkeys were given a slight nick with a knife and tied upside down to bleed slowly to death; but as I've said if it makes the meat better and animals don't have souls, what the heck!

For first-class value in the cruelty stakes, for the real tops in gruesome entertainment and haute cuisine, forget pigs, turkeys and crimped salmon, for it was damn nigh impossible to beat the good old feathered funster *Branta Brenicula*, the goose. Now geese have the good fortune – though some might question this expression – to have livers which can absorb enormous quantities of fat before the bird steatifies into an oily cadaver, and from this liver is made a delicacy called pâté de fois gras. Now geese kept under normal conditions, allowed to graze and flap around, don't develop this oily liver as they simply work off their excess carbohydrates in grazing and seeking out food. So to prevent the geese flapping off their surplus energy instead of turning it into an oily gooey liver, goose-fatteners nailed their geese to the floor of fattening rooms and pints of damp grain mash, mash laced with gin to get the bird sleepy and hasten the fattening process (and also to flavour the flesh) were pumped down the bird's throat by means of a mechanical goose crammer. Even hens were not spared this indignity and agony as Christmas approached. French-trained goose-fatteners, for the French had the knack of making pâté de fois gras down to a fine art, went that teensy-weensy bit further to fatten the liver of their geese. Birds, owls excepted, are reluctant to move around after dark and hence what is known in the scientific world as their katabolic rate slows down to near zero or in layman's terms the bird fattens more quickly in darkness. So some enterprising Gaulois came up with a great little notion to get his geese to fatten more quickly, and pricked out his wards' bright blue and quite appealing eyes with a pin, allowing them to fatten in total darkness, the monotony of which was broken only by the sound of some inhumane fiend pumping grain down the birds' gullets. 'Vive la France'? 'Vive la difference' say I, except that there was no difference. We would have done it as well if we'd have thought of it, but the French are credited with being the first in their field in the gentle art of goose blinding.

However even if one's appetite doesn't extend to the flesh of geese, good old *Branta Brenicula* and his allied forms could still brighten up the fast-fading days of summer by being lead player in a neat little game called 'goose pulling'. In Scotland, an area never really famed for its inhuman cruelty, as for instance was and possibly is the Midlands, the goose pulling was a popular sport's day in the eighteenth century. Here a goose was suspended head down from a gibbet and left fluttering while various horsemen rode past trying to snatch off the goose's head. Mind you the goose's head was well greased, which I admit didn't minimise the cruelty of the activity, but certainly brightened up the game a little. Don't knock this neat little gig as being unEnglish just because it started in Scotland, for by 1750 the activity had caught on like wildfire in England; though, to be fair, not in East Anglia where geese were regarded as a bit special and were live plucked four times a year to get the goose feather beds, which the girl in the song left to join the Raggle Taggle Gypsies or was it the RSPCA, I can't quite remember now.

Yes, geese had a fairly rough time of it, though according to the horrid tale told by Rabelais, which I'm sure will be edited out, no one could accuse them of not being versatile creatures. Come to think of it Hans Andersen's 'Little Goose Girl' must have been a hardened little bitch, providing geese for such spectacles.

But if geese were perhaps the most tortured of God's creatures, cats were not far behind in the persecution stakes, and at certain times even overtook poor old *Branta Brenicula* for the title of the most crippled, maimed and tortured animal in Britain. Aside from the feat performed by the Beverley shepherd and that of the omnivore produced by the incredible Lord Barrymore, cats came in for considerable 'stick' from the British public. Stick it was, believe me, for one of the most popular entertainments in Britain at one time was the game of 'cat in the barrel'. Here a cat was placed in a barrel half-filled with soot, fresh soot for preference as it tends to burn the cat's eyes just a shade more, and the barrel rolled around a fair, while the audience, men and women and children alike, gave the barrel a hearty whack with a stick until the barrel burst and the cat escaped, whereupon the mob chased and killed the terrified beast with clubs. Pretty unpleasant if you ask me and a bit wasteful as well, for to get the best value from one's cat one should have tried a visit to the Tower menagerie, for when it was first opened visitors were allowed in free of charge if they brought with them a live cat and stuffed it through the bars of the lions' cage.

Boy oh boy, Britain must have seethed with nutters during the times which those less informed called the good old days. Good they may have been for people (typhoid, cholera and infant mortality excepted) but these times were pretty rough on poor dumb animals and scarcely a yokel in Britain during those days seems not to have either whacked a cat or done something unpleasant to a goose.

However, should one think that only the poor uneducated lower class went around beating eight bells out of cats or tearing greasy gooses' necks off, nothing could be further from the truth. Let me at once calm the readers' fears concerning this, by relating the tale of the Eton Ram Bait, as interesting an extra-curricular activity as ever designed by an educational establishment. Once a year a local butcher in Windsor on good terms with the school, but not on such good terms with local sheep, provided a live ram for the school's entertainment and the boys, who had probably whipped themselves into a state of excitement by the thought of such entertainment, promptly chased and whipped the ram, bludgeoning the life out of the wretched beast, chopping it to shreds, and making the body of the ram too mangled, bruised and mutilated for even the poor of the village to consider eating the flesh of the animal. Frequently the boys returned to the school happy but as covered with gore as one of Golding's boys in *Lord of the Flies*. So horrific was the spectacle of blood-stained boys hacking and tearing a ram to pieces, often with crowbars, or even bare hands, that few villagers turned out to watch the spectacle. Once, however, the ram – unsporting, as terrified sheep are wont to be – managed to outstrip its predators, swam the Thames and raced into Windsor market place to seek sanctuary under the stalls, whence it was dragged back to the school and ripped to pieces by the scholars; but this act so upset the townsfolk of Windsor that they complained to the head, who, rather than abolish this nasty little primitive ritual, decreed that the ram should be hamstrung (crippling it by severing the tendons in its ankles) to prevent it racing away and swimming the river again. Admittedly this monstrous little ceremony was abolished in 1747 possibly due to the antipathy of the population of Windsor rather than for humanitarian reasons, but up until the turn of the century it was nearly impossible to keep a dog or cat near Windsor because of the schoolboys' healthy interest in baiting and torturing animals, and lads from Harrow openly bought stolen cats to bait to death with bull terriers. It is interesting to note, poised as we are on the brink of a nuclear war, that most of our Prime Ministers were either Eton or Harrow educated!

Sickened by what you've read dear reader? Well, just stay with me, for the best, or most certainly the worst, is yet to come, for not only common folk and scholars couldn't resist a whack at dumb animals but even the godly seemed to have a yen to do something very unpleasant, to animals generally, and, in this case, to dogs in particular. In 1809 a Quaker, one not given to violence against his fellow man and so-called because he was so righteous that he 'quaked' in the fear of God, pleaded guilty at the Sussex Assizes to the nastiest crime imaginable. His neighbour had so upset this God-fearing upright man that he went and painted the sides and belly of his neighbour's pet dog with concentrated sulphuric acid to silence the beast. So efficacious was the remedy that two days later the dog ceased barking altogether for the bowels fell through the sides of the wretched creature. The jury were so shocked by the outrage that they ordered the culprit to pay a whole £5 note in damages, but no criminal action was taken against this monster – there was no law to prevent cruelty to animals, for if you remember, animals had no souls!

Cats, dogs, bulls, bears, geese (particularly geese) were treated abominably by our ancestors, and even our feathered friends were given some fearful treatment at the hands of people who professed to be sportsmen. During Victorian times it was a very profitable occupation to breed huge numbers of blue rock doves, birds very similar to our domesticated pigeons, to sell to sportsmen out to prove their virility by gunning down the odd bird or so. These doves were often so tame that when they were released to be shot at by 'sportsmen' – I'd question that term myself – they landed on the guns of their would be slayers and had to be driven into the air to allow gunmen a shot at them. However, should a terrified pigeon shooting straight into the air from out of its carrying box be too difficult a shot for the tyro sportsman, for a few pence a gunman eager to impress his young lady with his shooting prowess could tip the pigeon owner to incapacitate the pigeon by pulling out the feathers from one wing and either breaking or dislocating a pigeon's wings if the sportsman (that word again) was a simply rotten shot. Giddy young women, who at a time when it was fashionable to faint at the sight of a common or garden worm, cheered aloud when their beaux shot the heads off tame pigeons which toppled into the ladies' laps sprinkling their hair and gowns with blood. It's a funny old world mate, a funny old world. Of course this pigeon-shooting was abolished by the 1911 Act, but we still have a relic of the time in clay-pigeon shoots. True, these pigeons are made of pitch and wax, but let me assure you the originals were of flesh, blood and bone.

But for those too poor to own guns to blow helpless, hapless pigeons to pieces, all was not lost, for there was still the sport of sparrow mumpling. To those who don't understand the term sparrow mumpling, and I confess that before I researched this nasty tale I too was ignorant of the expression, Captain Francis Grose in his *Dictionary of the Vulgar Tongue* describes the sport admirably. At country fairs sparrows with their wings broken off to prevent escape were placed inside the crown of a hat and a contestant, who paid as much as ½d for his sport, invited to tie his hands behind his back and bite the head off the crippled sparrow. Sometimes the sparrow managed to get in the odd peck or two before it was decapitated, but there is a fly in every ointment and not only is no sport without its little disadvantages but sparrows are well known for being unsporting little sods.

In time a society called the Society for the Prevention of Cruelty to Animals later to be given Royal patronage, hence the abbreviation RSPCA, was formed to prevent such atrocities and in 1802 a bill was passed to abolish baiting sports, seemingly a great step forward except that the wording of the bill was so loose and sloppy that bull-baiting, the only commonly practised baiting sport now that bears were becoming a little too rare or a little too costly to chop, rip, maim, blind and cripple, was excluded from the bill. However in 1835 another bill was passed and thus the sport became a thing of the past. It had started in 1209 in Stamford and here too it died, for in 1837 the Mayor of Stamford in defiance of the law allowed a really rowdy bull-bait, with dogs, ruffians, the whole bag of tricks, to be staged in the main streets in defiance of the decision of the Lincoln Assizes, and the whole rowdy crowd of fiends was dispersed by cavalry. The crowd probably received a lot of sore heads and broken bones and the mayor a bill for £600, and that was that – the end of bull-baiting.

The act did a lot of good for mankind generally (bulls certainly appreciated it) for gradually a new type of man seemed to come into being, a man more sensitive to the needs of beasts, less enthusiastic about whacking cats in barrels of soot or pulling the greased heads off geese, a man who thought before he poured vitriol over the sides of his neighbour's dog – well, that's how the theory goes. In practice things certainly haven't turned out quite as expected. Baiting is rare these days, though the introduction of a particularly game type of bull terrier called the American Pit bull terrier has given the sport of badger-baiting a sudden, and let us hope a temporary revival. Dog fighting is heard of now and again, as is cockfighting, but such stories are usually exaggerated out of proportion by the media, and a sale of game birds staged at Lambourn Lurcher Show in 1982 suddenly became a full blooded main (according to the press that is) with a spot of badger-baiting thrown in for good measure. Lambourn became a St Bartholemew's Fair according to the papers, and the natives of the town shut the show down, but it's questionable whether the temperament of the British people has changed all that much or the vicious streak we all seem to possess has merely been kept in check by fairly vigorous laws. The typical Britisher is just as cruel and insensitive as he ever was if you ask me, and now and again prosecutions highlight an atrocity which illustrates this point.

Just look at the way the average man in the street treats his pets, disposing of them in the most barbarous manner when ever his fancy takes him. Come summer holidays some of the lengths of canals which criss-cross the Midlands are practically impassable, becoming a foul-smelling Sargasso sea of fur, feather and putrescence where dogs, cats and pigeons have struggled and fluttered their way to watery graves when their owners decided 'It's Majorca for us this year'. True, the owners will return wearing sombreros and carrying little furry toy donkeys and start keeping livestock as soon as they settle in, but next year it will be the same again. Have you seen that advert the RSPCA put on TV in early December, begging and pleading with the public not to buy a puppy or kitten as Christmas presents? Heed their advice, and breeders of such creatures should certainly not turn off Christmas-market litters. Bank Holiday August invariably finds the M5 almost blocked with the cadavers of unwanted dogs, all roughly ten months old, all products of 'Guess what Mummy's buying you for Christmas, love' and 'Guess what Mummy's grown tired of, my darling.' It's an unkind world out there I'm sure and kids should be taught of the existence of it by horrid parables and fairy stories, just as Jesus showed the inconsistencies of state and religion by equally simple stories. Teachers don't do their duty to kids by telling them of a twee little world of respectability and kindness which exists just over the catchment area. Kids should be told that as soon as Santa has finished his Yuletime run he gets thoroughly pissed off with his now useless reindeers and butchers them, salting them down for the sultry Greenland summer, and that next year a brand new set of Donners and Blitzens, Prancers and Dancers gallop their way on the present-giving run, hell-bent for the New Year and the Knacker's Yard.

Come to think of it there must be an enormous market for products which will snuff out unwanted pets of which parents and kids have grown weary, and sooner or later some firm is bound to latch on to the idea, and one day soon packets of 'Hamster slay' and 'Gerbicide' will festoon the pet-shop shelves, packets which will bear twee little instruction pamphlets reading 'A few drops on Tiny or Tuffy or Fluffy's food will render him a rigid stiff cadaver, ready for burying in moments'. Or how about 'Fish Rid' for those those who have tired of their sets of soothing tropicals – 'a few crystals sprinkled on the water's surface' will enable the weary fish keeper to flush the whole lot, plastic Neptune and his fairy grot as well, down the loo, 'and this is just one of our products in the Disposipets Range'. A nation of animal lovers – you've got to be kidding.